Small
Teaching

Small Teaching

Everyday Lessons From the Science of Learning

James M. Lang

JOSSEY-BASS™
A Wiley Brand

Published by Jossey-Bass
A Wiley Brand
One Montgomery Street, Suite 1000, San Francisco, CA 94104-4594—www.josseybass.com

Jossey-Bass books and products are available through most bookstores. To contact Jossey-Bass directly call our Customer Care Department within the U.S. at 800-956-7739, outside the U.S. at 317-572-3986, or fax 317-572-4002.

Wiley publishes in a variety of print and electronic formats and by print-on-demand. Some material included with standard print versions of this book may not be included in e-books or in print-on-demand. If this book refers to media such as a CD or DVD that is not included in the version you purchased, you may download this material at http://booksupport.wiley.com. For more information about Wiley products, visit www.wiley.com.

Library of Congress Cataloging-in-Publication Data

ISBN 978-1-118-94449-3 (Hardcover)
ISBN 978-1-118-94451-6 (ePDF)
ISBN 978-1-118-94450-9 (ePub)

Cover design by: Wiley

Printed in the United States of America
FIRST EDITION

HB Printing   V10010431_052219
PB Printing

For Katie, Madeleine, Jillian, Lucie, and Jack,
who taught me much when they were small

Contents

Acknowledgments

First and foremost, I must express my gratitude for monthly writer's group meetings with Mike Land and Sarah Cavanagh, during which I received incredibly wise and helpful feedback on every chapter of this book. Mike and Sarah served perfectly as advanced and interested readers, and they made this a better book in every way possible. Special thanks to Sarah for helping me avoid glaring errors in my use of terminology and theories from her home discipline of psychology and for pointing me to numerous articles that helped thicken my research.

I had the opportunity to present the research from this book—and to test out its applicability to instructors—at many colleges and universities while I was drafting and revising the manuscript. So thanks to my hosts and workshop participants at Olds College (Canada), Misericordia University, Regis College, the University of Denver, Fisher College, Florida Institute of Technology, King's Academy (Jordan), MacEwan University (Canada), Indiana State University, the DeLange Conference at Rice University, the University of Texas–San Antonio Health Sciences College, Bucknell University, Georgia Tech, and Columbus State Community College.

The seeds for this book were first planted at a meeting with David Brightman at the Teaching Professor Conference in New Orleans, and he was an excellent guide as I worked my way through the conception and proposal stages. His commitment to higher education and to publishing excellent books made him an ideal editor. Pete Gaughan and Connor O'Brien proved equally dedicated to the project, and my thanks especially to Connor for his developmental notes on the first draft of the book. Two outside reviewers also helped improve the book in many important ways, and I am grateful to them as well.

Assumption College gave me the sabbatical that enabled me to draft the book and to meet my deadlines, and many colleagues there, both faculty and administrative, have been supportive of my work.

I wrote the vast majority of this book at Nu Café in Worcester, Massachusetts. Thanks for all the green tea. It seemed to help.

I come from a family of teachers; it must have been something in the water where we grew up. I continue to find inspiration especially from my sister, Peggy, who has served as both teacher and principal to urban student populations in Chicago, and from my brother, Tony, at whose heels I have been tagging along as a student and teacher and writer and human being since we were childhood bunkmates.

Much of my extracurricular thinking about learning happens as a result of observing the experiences of my children, to whom this book is dedicated, so thanks to them for the enthusiasm they have always shown for learning both in and out of school.

Even more of my thinking about education happens as a result of my conversations with my wife, an elementary school teacher. During part of the time that I was writing this book I spent Friday mornings volunteering in her kindergarten classroom, and I was reminded each week of the incredible value of teaching as a profession and of the selfless commitment that so many teachers make to their students. Those reminders continually renewed my inspiration to write this book.

So a final and most heartfelt thanks to Anne—for everything.

About the Author

James M. Lang is professor of English and director of the Center for Teaching Excellence at Assumption College in Worcester, MA. He is the author of four books: *Cheating Lessons: Learning From Academic Dishonesty* (Harvard University Press, 2013), *On Course: A Week-by-Week Guide to Your First Semester of College Teaching* (Harvard University Press, 2008), *Life on the Tenure Track: Lessons From the First Year* (Johns Hopkins University Press, 2005), and *Learning Sickness: A Year with Crohn's Disease* (Capital Books, 2004). He writes a monthly column on teaching and learning for the *Chronicle of Higher Education*; his work has been appearing in the *Chronicle* since 1999. His book reviews and public scholarship on higher education have appeared in a wide variety of newspapers and magazines, including the *Boston Globe*, *Chicago Tribune*, and *Time*. He is a member of the Fulbright Senior Specialist roster in higher education, and he has conducted workshops on teaching for instructors at more than 50 colleges or universities in the United States and abroad. He has a BA in English and philosophy from the University of Notre Dame, an MA in English from St. Louis University, and a PhD in English from Northwestern University. Visit his website at http://www.jamesmlang.com.

Small Teaching

> "Much of what we've been doing as teachers and students isn't serving us well, but some comparatively simple changes could make a big difference". (9)
>
> **Make It Stick: The Science of Successful Learning**

I n October 2014, fans of American major league baseball relished the sight of the plucky Kansas City Royals fighting their way to the final game of the World Series. What captured the attention of so many baseball enthusiasts was that the key to the Royals' success throughout the season had been an old-fashioned approach to the sport called small ball. Rather than relying on muscle-bound sluggers hitting grand slam home runs, the Royals instead utilized the simple, incremental strategies that enable baseball teams to move runners from one base to the next and keep the other team from scoring: bunting, stealing bases, hitting sacrifice fly balls, and playing solid defense. These unglamorous achievements on the field don't win baseball players the accolades that they might earn from smashing towering, game-winning home runs, but teams who play small ball in concerted and effective ways don't need those kinds of dramatic heroics. Indeed, some baseball analysts pointed to the success of the Royals, who achieved their victories on a relatively small budget, as evidence of the future of baseball. "The Royals have found a winning formula," wrote Sean Gregory, the baseball columnist for *Time* magazine. "These days, if you swing for the fences, you're more likely than ever to strike out. So just put the ball in play … and take your chances with your legs. Steal bases to eke out those diminishing runs. Small-ball is cheap, and effective. This is where the game is headed" (Gregory 2014b). As the article notes, the really wonderful feature of small ball is that it's both effective and inexpensive—and hence available to everyone. Even teams that spend money on those glamorous sluggers can still play small ball—as was evidenced in the final game of the World Series, in which the bigger budget San Francisco Giants snatched victory from the Royals by beating them at their own game and scoring two of their three runs on unglamorous sacrifice fly balls (Gregory 2014a).

My own acquaintance with small ball comes from a less dramatic story than the one the Kansas City Royals engineered in fall 2014. I have five children and live in a New England city where love for baseball runs deep. So for the past 15 years I have been sitting on uncomfortable metal benches for 2 months every late spring and watching my children play various levels of softball and baseball in our city leagues. The particular league to which my children belong is a long-standing one; many of the coaches played in the league when they were children. These coaches frequently take the games quite seriously, perhaps in an effort to recapture the glory of their childhood playing days. As a result, they scout and select the best players every year who are coming up from the younger leagues and thus leave newer or inexperienced coaches to draft their teams from a much depleted talent pool. Yet, despite the advantages that these more aggressive coaches gain in recruiting the top players, they don't always win. In little league as in the major leagues, the coaches who seem to have the greatest success are the ones who focus their attention—and the attention of their players—on mastering all of the small elements of the game. Small-ball coaches will signal their base runners to steal when the fielders are haphazardly tossing the ball around the infield, or they will ensure that someone is always backing up a throw to first base in case the first-base person misses. Since nobody is really bashing home runs out of the park on a softball team of 8-year-olds, small ball really represents the only guaranteed strategy for long-term success.

The idea for this book began to percolate at the end of one of those long softball seasons, as I was preparing for a round of fall visits to other college campuses in support of my previous book. I had been blessed for the past several years with invitations to present workshops for college instructors on teaching and learning in higher education at other institutions, an endeavor I welcomed and enjoyed. When I first began presenting, I relished the chance to speak to my fellow college and university teachers about major transformations they could make to their courses. Unfortunately, I was usually making such visits during the middle of a semester, which meant that workshop participants had to wait until the following semester to implement any of my suggestions. Even instructors with the best of intentions to revitalize their teaching might find it challenging to carry what they had learned about in a 2-hour workshop in October to their course planning in January or August, given all the work that would occupy their minds in the interim. More fundamentally, sudden and dramatic transformation to one's teaching is hard work and can prove a tough sell to instructors with so many time-consuming responsibilities. As a working instructor myself, I taught courses in literature and writing every semester, so I knew full well the depth of this challenge. As much as I frequently felt the urge to shake up my teaching practices with radical new innovations, I mostly didn't. Reconceiving your courses from the ground up takes time and energy that most of us have in short supply in the middle of the semester, and that we usually expend on our research during the semester breaks.

My reflections on this dilemma led me to consider whether I should incorporate into my workshops more activities that instructors could turn around and use in their classrooms the next morning or the next week without an extensive overhaul of their teaching—the pedagogical equivalents, in other words, of small ball. With that prospect in mind, I dove into the literature of teaching and learning in higher education with new eyes, seeking small-ball recommendations that were both easy to implement and well supported by the research. Over the course of many months this search led me through the work of cognitive psychologists who study the mechanics of learning, to neuroscientists and biologists who helped me understand some basic aspects of brain science, and to research in learning-related fields such as emotions and motivation. I was pleasantly surprised to find in these fields a manageable number of learning principles that seemed readily translatable into higher education classrooms. Gradually I began searching for practical examples of how these principles could operate in the classroom, and I began recommending some of the strategies I was discovering to participants in my workshops. I could feel the energy and excitement rising in the room whenever participants could see a short road between a late afternoon workshop and a concrete and positive change that they could make in their classes the next morning. But nothing made me more interested and excited than the small successes I experienced when I incorporated some of the strategies I had learned about into my own classroom. Over the course of that fall semester, as I both worked on my own teaching and spoke with other instructors about these ideas, I became convinced of the seemingly paradoxical notion that fundamental pedagogical improvement was possible through incremental change—in the same way that winning the World Series was possible through stealing bases and hitting sacrifice fly balls.

This newfound conviction ultimately gave rise to the notion of *small teaching*, an approach that seeks to spark positive change in higher education through small but powerful modifications to our course design and teaching practices. Small teaching as a fully developed strategy draws from the deep well of research on learning and higher education to create a deliberate, structured, and incremental approach to changing our courses for the better. The past several decades have brought us a growing body of research on how human beings learn, and a new generation of scholars in those fields has begun to translate findings from the laboratories of memory and cognition researchers to the higher education classrooms of today. Their findings increasingly suggest the potency of small shifts in how we design our courses, conduct our classrooms, and communicate with our students. Some of the findings may also suggest pathways to change that arise from dramatic transformation to our courses, and I will point toward a few of these in this book's final chapter. But if we are seeking to boost our students' learning of course content, to improve their basic intellectual skills—such as writing, speaking, and critical thinking—and to prepare them for success in their careers, then I believe we can find in small teaching an approach to our shared work of educating students that is effective for our students and accessible to the largest number of working college and university teachers.

Widespread accessibility to working teachers matters a great deal, especially if we consider the incredibly diverse range of contexts in which higher education operates these days. Teaching innovations that have the potential to spur broad changes must be as accessible to underpaid and overworked adjuncts as they are to tenured faculty at research universities. They must find a home on the campus of a small liberal arts college as easily as they do on the commuter campuses of regional comprehensives. They must offer something to traditional lecturers in big rooms and to discussion leaders in small seminars. The activities outlined in this book, taken as a whole, fulfill these directives: with a little bit of creative thinking, they can translate into every conceivable type of teaching environment in higher education, from lectures in cavernous classrooms to discussions in small seminar rooms, from fully face-to-face to fully online courses and every blended shade between. They stem from very basic principles of how human beings learn and hence cross both discipline and content type—whether you are teaching students to memorize facts or formulae, to develop their speaking skills, or to solve complex problems. Not every instructor in every discipline in every teaching context will find a space for all of the small teaching activities outlined here, but every reader should find opportunities to use at least some of them. You can implement them tomorrow morning, next week on Friday, in the design of your next quiz or test, and even—as we shall see in the final part of the book—in the next e-mail you send to your students.

To ensure that these techniques lent themselves to this kind of universal accessibility, and thus merit space beneath the umbrella of small teaching, the principles outlined in this book had to meet three basic criteria. First, they had to have some foundation in the learning sciences. Fortunately, over the past decade or two a cohort of learning scientists has begun to present findings from those disciplines in forms that are accessible to nonspecialists like me. Books like Daniel Schacter's *The Seven Sins of Memory*; Daniel Willingham's *Why Don't Students Like School*; or Peter Brown, Henry Roediger, and Mark McDaniel's *Make It Stick* present the results of research in neuroscience and cognitive theory in ways that spell out their implications clearly for teachers and learners. Second, these learning principles had to have a positive impact in real-world educational environments— higher education whenever possible. This test proved the most challenging one to meet; some strategies that seemed plausible to me, or that stemmed from fascinating laboratory experiments, did not ultimately make it into the book since they could not clear this essential hurdle. Finally, I had to observe the principles directly myself somehow, either from my own experiences as a teacher or learner or from direct observation of other teaching and learning environments. Call me overly cautious, but I needed these principles to pass this final smell test for me to be absolutely certain that I could recommend them to working instructors. Most of the chapters that follow begin with an example of how I have sniffed out these principles in some learning experience from my own life or from the lives of my students or even my children, and I hope these personal examples might help you identify moments in which you have seen them at work in your own learning histories as well.

Assuming a teaching and learning activity met all three of these criteria, it still had to be capable of implementation in ways that fell under the umbrella of small teaching. As you will find in the pages that follow, a small teaching approach or activity may take one of three forms:

- **Brief (5–10-minute) classroom or online learning activities.** I love the idea of small interventions in a learning session that can capture (or recapture) the attention of students, provide quick opportunities for student engagement, and introduce or seal up new learning. Even when you have an otherwise busy class session planned, you can find time for a 5-minute activity that will provide a substantive boost to the learning of your students.
- **One-time interventions in a course.** As in the case of the Minute Thesis exercise in Chapter 4, the meaning of *small* will

occasionally shift from "a small portion of a class" to "a small portion of the course." In other words, some small teaching activities could occupy an entire class period but need to do so only a single time in the semester.

· **Small modifications in course design or communication with your students.** These recommendations might not translate directly into 10-minute or one-time activities, but they also do not require radical rethinking of your courses. They might inspire tweaks or small changes in the way you organize the daily schedule of your course, write your course description or assignment sheets, or respond to the writing of your students. The strategies in Part III especially will fit under this category of small teaching approaches.

An essential shared quality of all three of these forms of small teaching is that they *require minimal preparation and grading*. Although we are all busy, this feature of small teaching strikes me as especially important for adjunct instructors, who may be teaching multiple courses on different campuses or working additional jobs to make ends meet. An adjunct instructor who can walk into class every day with a variety of small teaching exercises can actually reduce overall preparation time by seeding these powerful learning activities throughout her teaching. One-time activities like the Minute Thesis or a mindful practice session, which likewise require minimal preparation or grading, can also serve as a back pocket technique that an instructor could use on a day when a sick child or medical emergency or mental health day has reduced or eliminated normal preparation time.

Yet such activities, which may first find their way into your classroom as a means of filling an empty 10 minutes at the end of class or an unplanned course session, have the power to produce as much or more learning than your anxiously overprepared lecture. For me, this represents the real power and promise of small teaching. I hope the chapters that follow will demonstrate to you that small teaching is not a realist's compromise, an inferior choice we have to make because we don't have the time or energy to make the big changes that would *really* make a difference to our students. We have excellent evidence of the learning power of small teaching activities—in study after study, as you will see in the chapters that follow, small teaching activities have been proven to raise student performance on learning tasks by the equivalent of a full letter grade or higher. That's powerful evidence—as powerful as anything I have seen in the learning research, including in studies devoted to grand slam approaches that grab the headlines of the *Chronicle of Higher Education* or other publications of our profession.

In further service to the argument that small and incremental approaches can have great power (and to the fact that we are all busy), you will find a variety of levels at which you can understand the small teaching strategies recommended in each chapter. You will have the richest understanding of any given small teaching approach by reading the chapter in its entirety, of course, but you can also drop into the practical application sections in the latter half of the chapters if you are looking for fast and immediate help. The structure of each chapter includes the following elements:

- **Introduction:** You will usually find here examples of how the particular learning phenomenon described in that chapter might appear in everyday life.
- **In Theory:** This section delves into the research that supports the recommendations of the chapter and includes descriptions of experiments from laboratories and classrooms as well as brief descriptions of key findings or principles from the cognitive sciences.
- **Models:** Four or five detailed models are described in each chapter—fully fleshed-out examples of how instructors could

incorporate a small teaching approach into their course design, classroom or online practice, or communication with students.

· **Principles:** I hope and expect that instructors will not simply follow the models but also will take the overall strategy and develop their own new models. The principles provide guidance for creating your own small teaching strategies.

· **Quick Small Teaching:** One-sentence reminders of the simplest means of putting the small teaching strategy of that chapter into practice; flip through or return to these when you have 15 minutes before class and need a quick tip for an engaged learning activity.

· **Conclusion:** A final reflection on the main theory or strategy of the chapter.

I hope that your first reading of each chapter will help you see immediately how to make changes to your teaching that will benefit your students. But I hope as well that you can continue to rely on the book long after your first reading. Keep it handy and flip through it every now and again or whenever you feel the need to try something new and different in your classroom. Use the book to spark new or newly invigorated conversations on your campus about how we can best help our students learn and about how we can best promote positive change in higher education. Finally, when you are ready to explore further the literature on teaching and learning in higher education, and move beyond these specific recommendations, page through the Works Cited list for more reading ideas. I have attempted to keep that list as small as possible, in order not to overwhelm new readers to this field, and to focus on some key texts and seminal studies that are easily accessible to most readers. (Know that the field of research for every chapter topic in this book extends far beyond my spare citations.)

The small teaching models and principles that you will find in the chapters ahead can be taken singly, as one-time spurs to innovation in a specific course session or unit plan, but they could also be combined to create an entirely new approach to your teaching. If you are reading this book over a break, while you are not teaching, see if you can draw systematically from each of the three major parts of the book as you plan your next course, creating a comprehensive strategy for boosting student learning in your classroom. But if you are reading it during the middle of the semester, shift your focus from the forest to the trees. Select one activity or course modification, and commit to it for the rest of the semester. Make sure you give new activities time to flower; nothing works exactly as we might hope it would on the first attempt, so it might take several iterations before activities like opening or closing prediction exercises really begin to pay dividends. And as I will argue in the conclusion, search for ways to evaluate the effects of your small teaching changes, and determine whether they belong in your permanent teaching repertoire. Enlist the help of the teaching and learning center on your campus, if you have one, to help you better understand how to measure the impact of specific changes to your teaching on student learning. Students are not the only ones who will benefit from new learning as the result of small teaching, in other words; you can use these activities to take a more systematic approach to your own teaching, thinking deliberately about implementing, measuring, and modifying a range of possible teaching strategies in ways that will keep you learning and growing as a teacher throughout your career.

But we shouldn't get too far ahead of ourselves, and worry yet about your whole career. I will assume that you have class tomorrow, or next Monday, or at least within the next month or two, and you're looking for ideas.

Let's begin small.

Part I

Knowledge

I magine the media storm that erupted in 1956 upon the publication of an educational book with the attention-grabbing title of *Taxonomy of Educational Objectives: The Classification of Educational Goals, Handbook I: Cognitive Domain*. The author of this spine tingler was psychologist Benjamin Bloom, who sought to articulate a set of objectives that teachers could use to guide their instructional activities. In spite of its eye-glazing title, the book's content ultimately became a sacred text for educational theorists and administrators everywhere, giving them both a conceptual framework and a vocabulary to articulate what they expected teachers could achieve in their classrooms. The taxonomy that Bloom created contains six major categories: Knowledge, Comprehension, Application, Analysis, Synthesis, and Evaluation. A quick glance over the six categories would suggest that they follow a progression from lower to higher orders of complexity, from a static possession of knowledge to more creative forms of thinking in the categories of synthesis and evaluation. Indeed, the taxonomy is often depicted in the shape of a pyramid, with knowledge at the bottom and evaluation or creation at the apex.

Unfortunately, this visual image of Bloom's taxonomy as a pyramid, which all teachers have likely encountered at some point in their lives, has led many higher education instructors to view Bloom's categories in a distorted way. When you think of a pyramid, after all, where do you want to be? At the top, of course. Nobody wants to be down on the bottom row of a pyramid, crushed by the weight of the rising layers, unable to reach up for the stars. So some instructors seem to believe that the learning of facts or concepts, or helping students remember facts and concepts—or even procedures or basic skills—falls beneath them; they are interested only in higher order activities like critical thinking or making judgments or creating new knowledge. College instructors seem especially prone to this desire to hop over the bottom layer of the pyramid—or, more charitably, to assume either that elementary and secondary education should have helped students learn how to remember things or that students should master knowledge outside of class and thus that class time can be exclusively devoted to higher cognitive activities. In recent years such instructors have used a new argument to justify their dismissal of the knowledge category of Bloom's taxonomy: the omnipresence of Google. Why should we bother to help students remember facts, so this argument runs, when all of the facts of the entire world are available to them at the touch of a fingertip? Facts now come in the form of smartphones, and most of our students—at least in developed economies—have one or at the very least some form of regular access to the Internet. Let the Internet provide them with the facts, and we will instead focus our energies on the higher cognitive activities that make use of those facts.

Appealing though it might be to offload the responsibility for teaching our students basic knowledge to their elementary school teachers or to Google, the research of cognitive psychologists who study learning and the basic study habits of most students suggest that we cannot do this. One of our first and most important tasks as teachers is to help students develop a rich body of knowledge in our content areas—without doing so, we handicap considerably their ability to engage in cognitive activities like thinking and evaluating and creating. As cognitive psychologist Daniel Willingham argued, you can't think creatively about information unless you have information in your head to think about. "Research from cognitive science has shown," he explained, "that the sorts of skills that teachers want for their students—such as the ability to analyze and think critically—*require* extensive factual knowledge" (Willingham 2009, p. 25). We have to know things, in other words, to think critically about them. Without any information readily available to us in our brains, we tend to see new facts (from our Google searches) in isolated, noncontextual ways that lead to shallow thinking. Facts are related to other facts, and the more of those relationships we can see, the more we will prove capable of critical analysis and creative thinking. Students who don't bother to memorize anything will never get much beyond skating over the surface of a topic.

But the issue runs more deeply than this. When we learn new facts, we are building up mental structures that enable us to process and organize the next set of new facts more effectively. Knowledge is foundational: we won't have the structures in place to do deep thinking if we haven't spent time mastering a body of knowledge related to that thinking. The depiction of Bloom's taxonomy as a pyramid actually does acknowledge this important principle; one cannot get to the top levels of creative and critical thinking, after all, without a broad and solid foundation of knowledge beneath them. As Willingham put it, "Thinking well requires knowing facts, and that's true not simply because you need something to think *about*. The very processes that teachers care most about—critical thinking processes such as reasoning and problem-solving—are intimately intertwined with factual knowledge that is stored in long-term memory (not just found in the environment)" (Willingham 2009, p. 28).

As a simple illustration of the intertwinement of facts and thinking, consider the example of a trial lawyer who has to build an argument over the course of a trial, responding on short notice to witnesses or actions by the judge. We might think about a lawyer who works skillfully in such a situation as an adept and creative thinker, one who can respond quickly on her feet and construct arguments with facility. But if we listen to her making those arguments, we are likely to hear lots and lots of facts: legal principles, examples from other famous cases, statements from other witnesses, and so on. Undoubtedly, the lawyer in this case demonstrates complex cognitive and creative skills in building arguments from all of those facts, but no such thinking will arise without those facts. More important, the lawyer's gradual mastery of a body of facts, over the course of years of study and legal practice, enables her to take what she is encountering in this trial and invest it with meaning by connecting it with previous cases and trials, thus better preparing her for her next round of critical thinking in the courtroom. Likewise, I know that if I ask students to think critically about the meaning of a Romantic poem in my literature survey course, the student with a deep factual knowledge of the historical context in which it was written will offer me a better analysis than the one who just eyeballs it and Googles a few facts at random. We need factual material in our memory for every cognitive skill we might want to teach our students.

We also cannot assume that students are perfectly capable of memorizing such information on their own. In fact, research on student learning strategies suggests that students typically make poor choices when they attempt to learn new information—and that they make those choices even when they know better. Brown, Roediger, and McDaniel, the authors of *Make it Stick: The Science of Successful Learning*, described a fascinating experiment in which students were given two different strategies for learning how to identify characteristics of the work of different painters: studying the paintings either in similar groups (i.e., *massed* studying) or all mixed together (i.e., *interleaved* studying). The students who studied the paintings in interleaved fashion performed better on tests they took after their study periods—but this did not seem to make a difference in how they thought about studying, as the authors explained: "Despite [the] results, the students who participated in these experiments persisted in preferring massed practice, convinced that it served them better. Even after they took the test and could have realized from their own performance that interleaving was the better strategy for learning, they clung to their belief that the concentrated viewing of paintings by one artist was better" (Brown, Roediger, and McDaniel 2014, p. 54).

In other words, these students continued to believe in the superior power of a study strategy that had just been demonstrated to them as less effective than a simple alternative! Like all of us, these students suffered from biases and misconceptions about learning and how it works. Tell students to study for a test, and most of them will pull out their notebooks or textbooks and read them over and over again, despite scads of research telling us that this is just about the least effective learning strategy for mastering a new body of information. Even if students have encountered this research or have been taught effective study strategies by previous teachers, they still are likely to persist in ineffective learning strategies.

Hence, if we care about students having knowledge that they can use to practice their higher order cognitive skills, we should help them acquire that knowledge. We might rightly not want to spend an extraordinary amount of time and energy on this aspect of their learning, which is what makes it such a perfect realm for small teaching. As you will read in what follows, small teaching activities leveraged into the first and final minutes of a class session can provide a powerful boost to student mastery of knowledge; so, too, can simple tweaks to the organization of your course and the order in which you introduce new material and review older material. Taking advantage of these easy opportunities to help students remember course material will ensure that students can engage more deeply and meaningfully in the complex learning tasks to which you want to devote more of your time and energy—and to which we give more full consideration in Part II.

Chapter 1

Retrieving

INTRODUCTION

I wrote almost every word of this book sitting in a coffee shop about two blocks from my home. Most weekdays I would walk in, find a spot near an electrical outlet, fire up my laptop, and then head to the counter to order my beverage. I am a person of routines when it comes to food and drink, so every day for about 6 months I placed the same order: medium green tea. The coffee shop had its routines as well, which meant that most of the time I was placing my order with the same young woman. Yet in spite of the fact that she saw my smiling face 3 or 4 days a week making the same order, she always looked up at me expectantly when I arrived, as if I had not requested the same thing a hundred times before. She would even ask me the same two questions about my tea order every time: "Hot or cold?" "Honey or lemon?" Hot and No. Every time. As the weeks and months of this stretched on, it became a mild source of amusement to me to see if she would ever remember my order. She never did. Until, that is, I walked in one day and felt a little mischievous.

"Can I help you?" she said.

"Can you guess?" I replied.

She looked up as if seeing me for the first time, and she smiled sheepishly.

"Oh gosh," she said. "Why am I blanking?"

"It's OK," I said. "No problem. Medium green tea. Hot, nothing in it."

The next time I showed up at the coffee shop was a couple of days later. I walked in, found my spot, fired up the laptop, and approached my forgetful friend at the counter. To my astonishment, she pointed at me with a smile and said:

"Medium green tea, hot, no honey or lemon?"

This little story illustrates perfectly a learning phenomenon called the retrieval effect (and sometimes also called the testing effect). Put as simply as possible, the retrieval effect means that if you want to retrieve knowledge from your memory, you have to practice retrieving knowledge from your memory. The more times that you practice remembering something, the more capable you become of remembering that thing in the future. Every time I walked into that coffee shop and told the barista my order, she was receiving the information afresh from me; she did not have to draw it from her memory. She was doing the student equivalent of staring at her notes over and over again—a practice that cognitive psychologists will tell you is just about the most ineffective study strategy students can undertake. When I made one very small change to our interaction by "testing" her to remember my order—even though she didn't get it right—she had to practice, for the first time, drawing that piece of information from her memory. And because it was such a simple piece of information, one practice was enough to help her remember it for the next time. It won't be quite as simple for our students, who have to remember more complex stuff than my order at the coffee shop. But the principle is exactly the same. The more times any of us practice remembering something we are trying to learn, the more firmly we lodge it in our memories for the long term.

This retrieval effect has been the subject of multiple articles in the popular press in recent years, as research findings from cognitive scientists jump from their laboratories into the laps of journalists and popular education writers. But folk psychological awareness of this phenomenon has been around since the time of the ancient Greeks. The philosopher Aristotle was describing it when he said in his essay "On Memory," that "exercise in repeatedly recalling a thing strengthens the memory" (cited in Brown, Roediger, and McDaniel 2014, p. 28). With his use of the words *exercise* and *strengthen* he also initiated a long tradition, now frequently repeated in articles on the retrieval effect in the popular press, of thinking about the brain like a muscle. This comparison helps illustrate the fact that memory practice improves memory skills in the same way that swimming practice improves swimming skills. However, this analogy also has the potential to horrify your neuroscience friends because the physical organ of the brain is totally unlike a muscle. But if we can limit ourselves to the statement that training yourself to remember something resembles training a muscle to do something, in the very limited sense that both require frequent and deliberate practice (or exercise), we can let it stand.

The retrieval effect is also sometimes called the testing effect as a way to help teachers recognize its significance for student learning in their classrooms. Teachers (and students and parents) typically think about tests as a means to measure student learning. But tests, thought about in the most general way possible, are actually memory exercises. And if the research suggests that memory exercises improve our memories, that should mean that tests have the potential not just to measure learning but also actually to improve it. The problem with using the phrase *the testing effect* is that many of us have a very limited understanding of what the word *test* means—it recalls for us anxious students biting their pencil erasers as they sweat their way through a multiple-choice final exam. But of course testing can happen in a thousand different ways, from small daily quizzing exercises to oral examinations to online short-answer questions. The research that we will consider encompasses multiple types of these testing activities, all of which help students exercise their memory muscles to improve and solidify their knowledge base. Testing here simply means forcing learners to recall learned information, concepts, or skills from their memory. It can take the form of oral questioning in the opening 5 minutes of class just as easily as it can take the form of a high-stakes final exam. For that reason, I will continue to speak primarily of the retrieval effect and retrieval practice in what follows to avoid limiting your thinking about how you might manifest this teaching strategy in your classroom, and especially to help you think about how to implement retrieval practice through a variety of small teaching activities.

IN THEORY

The most recent, real-world experiments designed to illustrate the power of the retrieval effect have come from the Memory Lab of Henry L. Roediger at Washington University in St. Louis, which comprises the work of multiple researchers exploring the educational implications of their work on learning, cognition, and memory. As Roediger and his co-authors report in *Make It Stick: The Science of Successful Learning,* in 2006 researchers from the Memory Lab began working with a middle school in Columbia, Missouri, to see whether they could leverage the power of the retrieval effect in order to improve student learning (Brown, Roediger, and McDaniel 2014). Research associate Pooja K. Agarwal worked with a sixth-grade social studies teacher, Patrice Bain, to explore whether a structured set of retrieval practice activities in her six classes would help improve her students' learning. Rather than using retrieval practice with some of the classes and not with others, they divided the course material—standard-issue middle-school social studies textbook stuff, covering major world civilizations—into three groupings and treated each of those groupings differently. For the first set of material, the students were given three opportunities to practice retrieval in the form of regular quizzes, which were spaced out in the following way: one at the beginning of class, after they had read course material for homework but prior to the teacher discussing it; one at the end of class, after discussion of the material; and one just before each major test for the class. The teacher excused herself from the room during the quizzes; the students were shown the correct answers after they had given their answers, but the quizzes did not count toward their grades. For the second grouping of material, the students had the opportunity to restudy key concepts from the course that would appear on the exams. Bain covered the final grouping of material with her usual teaching methods, without any additional study or retrieval practice. It's worth noting, before discussing the results, that the additional retrieval practice did not come *in addition to* students' normal classroom time. It took place within the regular classroom hours, which means it was substituting for something else—lectures, or class discussions, or independent study time, or whatever else the teacher did on the nonquiz days. This deserves notice because some teachers might fear that retrieval practice will take time away from other, more important learning activities.

The experiment yielded, for our purposes, three important results. First and foremost, the authors explain, it demonstrated the potency of retrieval practice: "The kids scored a full grade level higher on the material that had been quizzed than on the material that had not been quizzed" (Brown, Roediger, and McDaniel 2014, p. 35). A year later the research group tried this same experiment in eighth-grade science courses at the same school, and the results were even stronger: "At the end of three semesters, the eighth graders averaged 79 percent (C+) on the science material that had not been quizzed, compared to 92 percent (A–) on the material that had been quizzed" (p. 35). A second important result was that the grades on the second grouping of material (for which the students had been given additional study time) were no better than the grades on the third grouping of the material (which had no special intervention at all). In other words, additional study time provided them with no additional learning benefit. "Mere re-reading," the authors conclude, "does not much help" (p. 35). Finally, and perhaps most importantly, the positive results of the experiment extended far out in time: "The testing effect persisted eight months later at the end-of-year exams" (p. 35). This has obvious implications for us as teachers; we want students to remember our course material beyond the initial testing period, and spaced-out retrieval practice (more on this spacing in Chapter 3) seems to have a powerful impact on long-term learning. But I can't leave this paragraph without highlighting these results one last time: a brief (and ungraded) multiple-choice quiz at the beginning and end of class and one additional quiz before the exam *raised the grades of the students by a full letter grade.*

Let's consider two more demonstrations of the power of retrieval practice before discussing the mechanics behind it and its translation into small teaching activities. The number of experiments in this area are rising dramatically each year, so we have many to choose from. However, I like an elegant demonstration of it by Roediger and Butler (2007) because it helps confirm what many readers might suspect: that not all types of testing are equal. In this experiment, Roediger and Butler had students observe three 30-minute lectures on art history, with slide shows, over a 3-day period. At the end of each lecture, students did one of four things: (a) take a short-answer test on the material they had just learned; (b) take a multiple-choice test on the material; (c) restudy some of the key facts from the lecture; or (d) walk out the door with no additional activity (which of course is what happens at the conclusion of most college classes). The students came back 30 days after the last of the three lectures to take a final short-answer test on the material; this time lapse created what the authors called "a more realistic timescale over which students may retain classroom lecture information prior to a test." In other words, students often learn material in class and are not tested on it until several weeks later; a final test thirty days after the learning period mimicked that longer interval (517). The students who took the short-answer tests directly after the lectures (a) scored the highest on the final exam, at 47%; the students who took multiple-choice exams (b) and had additional study time (c) scored about equally, at 36%; those who had no activity (d) scored around 20%. These numbers can seem a little disheartening, but keep in mind that in this experiment students had no reason or opportunity to revisit the course material during the 30-day interval between the lectures and the final exam—which, to a certain extent, makes the results of the students who took the short-answer exam really astonishing, since they recalled almost 50% of the material 30 days later with absolutely no reexposure or study time.

But this study helps us draw out some nuances. First, the students who performed the best were the ones who had to put the most active thought into their answers through short-answer questions. In the pithy formulation of Daniel Willingham, "Memory is the residue of thought" (Willingham, 2009, p. 54). Those short-answer questions required students to formulate answers in their own words, and hence to spend more time answering than the multiple-choice questions. Second, note that in this case the students who had the opportunity to engage in what the authors call "focused restudy" did perform better than the students who had no activity at all. I find this result somewhat heartening, because I have not spent my entire career using the kind of small teaching retrieval practice I am recommending in this chapter, and I would like to think that students who studied hard still learned something! So while some experiments, like our first one, have shown little difference between students who had extra study time and students who had no additional study or testing, this one yielded a different, more positive result. Third and finally, the students who scored the highest on the last short-answer test were the students who had taken previous short-answer tests. This could mean that the similarity in format between the two types of questions produced the better learning results. In other words, it may be that answering multiple-choice questions at the conclusion of a lesson produces one type of learning, and that type of learning does not translate well into performing well on short-answer questions.

To address that possibility, and to make a case for the special power of writing and problem-solving activities as a part of your retrieval practice, I want to consider one final experiment, this one conducted not by memory researchers in the laboratory but by the instructor in a real set of college chemistry courses. Brian Rogerson details in this study the result of an experiment he conducted over five semesters of teaching introductory chemistry at Richard Stockton College in New Jersey. During three of those semesters, which included his first year as a full-time faculty member, he taught using standard lecture techniques. During two of them, he made only one simple change to the course: 10 minutes before the end of each 75-minute class period, he stopped and asked students to respond to a question on the material he had just covered in the lecture. This question was the chemistry equivalent of a short-answer question, as you can see in this sample question he gives: "Give two reasons that K is more reactive than Li." Some of them required answers in the form of equations or formula, but all of them required more than just repetition from memory. The students wrote their answers down twice—once on a form that they returned to him and once on a paper to keep. This allowed Rogerson to review the answers prior to the next class—though he did not grade or return them—and then to address problems in their responses at the beginning of that next class session, with students able to check the answers they had given.

In the three semesters in which he did not conduct these end-of-class assessments (which he derived from Angelo and Cross's justly famous book *Classroom Assessment Techniques*) the rate of students who failed or withdrew from the course was 35%. In the semesters in which he used the technique, that rate fell to 17%. The number of Cs and Ds rose in the assessment semesters, which means that students who would have dropped were now performing at the C and D levels—not a miraculous transformation, but an impressive one nonetheless. The rates of A and B students stayed roughly stable in both cohorts, which may partially reflect the fact that an A or B student doesn't have as much room to improve as a C or D student does. Interestingly, in his introduction and discussion of this experiment, Rogerson made no mention of the possibility that retrieval practice may help explain the results of this experiment. Like most instructors who use assessments of any kind, he implemented it as a means to gauge the learning of his students and then saw it as an opportunity to provide feedback on their work. But you will note the similarity between the small task he required of his students and what the researchers in our last experiment required of their subjects: directly following the lecture, they asked students short questions about the material they had just covered. The results of such questions can be disheartening, as Rogerson pointed out: "Even after classes in which I felt I had explained something very well and thoroughly, there were students for whom the answer to the assessment was not obvious" (Rogerson 2003, p. 163). But even when students are frequently providing wrong answers, as they did for Rogerson and will do in your classes—and as long as you provide them feedback to help them correct their mistakes—the results of these experiments are hard to dismiss.

It remains for us only to note briefly why the retrieval effect works. The very short version is that memory researchers these days seem to believe that our long-term memories are capable of holding a huge amount of material. As cognitive psychologist Michelle Miller wrote in *Minds Online*, "There's wide consensus among memory researchers that long-term memory is essentially unlimited" (Miller 2014, p. 94). However, that unlimited storage capacity can be as much of a problem as a long-term memory with smaller storage capacity. In an earlier essay on what college teachers should know about memory, Miller explained that "in long-term-memory the limiting factor is not storage capacity, but rather the ability to find what you need when you need it. Long-term memory is rather like having a vast amount of closet space—it is easy to store many items, but it is difficult to retrieve the needed item in a timely fashion" (Miller 2011, p. 119). So the challenge for students, or for any of us, is not jamming facts and information down into our long-term memories but instead drawing those facts and information out when we need them or when they will help us in some way. Every time we extract a piece of information or an experience from our memory, we are strengthening neural pathways that lead from our long-term memory into our working memory, where we can use our memories to think and take actions. The more times we draw it from memory, the more deeply we carve out that pathway, and the more we make that piece of information or experience available to us in the future. So retrieval practice, in the form of either informal remembering of things, such as someone's order for a cup of green tea, or formal testing or quizzing in a school environment, as we saw in the aforementioned experiments, helps us pave the way for our memories to strengthen and improve.

MODELS

You don't have to think too hard about how to give your students effective retrieval practice; you just have to do it. The stumbling block for instructors arises less from designing strategies than from worrying about time: how much of their classroom or planning time do they want to devote to helping students remember foundational knowledge? Small teaching can come to the rescue here, as it can help instructors envision how to incorporate retrieval practice into bite-sized moments such as the opening and closing minutes of class and into small exercises in online or blended courses.

Opening Questions

The quickest method for cultivating retrieval practice in class takes the form of asking questions, either orally or in writing, about material that either you or the students have covered already. So instead of walking into class and providing an overview of what happened in the last class period or reminding students about the larger unit in which this particular class session is embedded, ask them to provide you with that information.

· Before we start, can anyone remind me what we talked about in class on Monday? How about what we were working on last week?
· Before I introduce the third major theory we will explore in the course, what have been the two main theories we have discussed thus far?
· We've seen several experiments in this area already this semester. Can someone remind me of the results we observed?

I should note from personal experience that if you have never tried this before, you might be surprised and disappointed at how difficult students will initially find such retrieval exercises. They will stare at you with jaws agape when you ask them about material you covered the day before yesterday—material you spent many hours preparing with care in your office. Take heart and persist. The more you do it, the better they will get it—and the better they get at it, the more deeply they are learning it. If you wish to formalize this type of activity, you could follow the lead of Annie Blazer: she begins each class with a single student providing a 3–5-minute summary of the previous class, and each student does this at least once per semester (Blazer 2014, p. 344).

Naturally, the same types of questions will work for material that students have read in advance of the class or for any homework problems they have completed. Again, prior to launching a lecture or course activity for the day, ask students to provide you with the highlights of the reading or work they have completed the night before. Students in my classes engage in brief writing exercises along these lines at the start of almost every class. When I started using these exercises, at the beginning of my teaching career, I knew nothing about the power of retrieval practice for learning. I implemented them for a very different reason: to help spark discussion. I had found that just walking into the room and asking students to engage in discussion of complex issues or questions did not work very well; it worked much more effectively if I posed a question, gave them 5 or 10 minutes to write a response, and *then* opened up the floor for discussion. But I also used them as a form of low-level quizzing, just to ensure that students were reading. Every question requires students to do a little bit of remembering and a little bit of thinking. If students have been assigned the first 75 pages of a novel for a class, for example, I might ask them to describe for me the primary qualities or characteristics of the narrator of the story. The word *primary* requires them to make some judgments about the variety of characteristics they might remember. Over the course of my 15 years of full-time teaching, I have come to recognize that these small writing exercises constitute the best method I have for supporting student learning in my courses—even if, as with most positive teaching experiences I have had, I stumbled upon this strategy through dumb luck or for the wrong reasons. Even though the students groan occasionally about the writing exercises over the course of the (long) semester, they note their value frequently both in conversation with me and in their evaluations of the course.

Brian Rogerson pointed out in his essay that one of the benefits of asking students to complete questions in writing, as opposed to just orally, is that it demands participation from all students. "These assessments," he wrote of his end-of-class questions, "attempt to survey all the students in the class, not just the more vocal ones as occurs when prompting the class for questions" (Rogerson 2003, p. 163). In other words, when you throw out your opening questions orally, you may be concerned that you are providing retrieval practice only for the students who habitually participate in class, thus leaving many other students without this benefit. However, this may not be the case. A memory experiment in which subjects were asked to view a map and to practice retrieval of the map's features *covertly* (i.e., simply by thinking about it and not speaking or writing any answers aloud) still showed boosts to their subsequent ability to reproduce the map from memory. This research suggests that "covert retrieval practice is as good as overt practice in benefitting later retention ... both methods produce a robust testing effect" (Pyc, Agarwal, and Roediger 2014, p. 80). Of course, this will work only if you provide the opportunity for covert retrieval, which means that you should ask questions, pause for a few moments to allow everyone to engage in retrieval practice, and then call on the student who has an answer at the ready. Even the students who don't speak the answer aloud can benefit from opening questions if they have a moment to think.

Closing Questions

Extrapolating from opening questions to closing questions doesn't take much creative thinking, and much of the research on retrieval practice—such as the experiment with those art history lectures—has focused on the effects of asking students questions about material they have just learned. So we know that closing questions are an effective small teaching strategy, and the same principles articulated before also apply here: focus on the key concepts that you want students to take away from the class session, and favor writing over oral questions whenever feasible. If you are using opening activities like prediction (discussed in the next chapter) or retrieval practice from the homework, and you have just one or two key concepts or ideas that you want them to take away from the class, you might consider asking the same question at the beginning and end of the class. If I asked my students at the beginning of class what they see as the primary characteristics of the narrator in the novel they read last night, and then we discussed that question and listed a bunch of characteristics on the board, I might conclude class by asking them to revisit and hone their judgment by writing a few final sentences for me on what they now see as the one most salient characteristic of the narrator. Likewise, if you ask students to make a prediction about course material you are about to present (an activity we will consider in the next chapter), you could conclude the class by asking them to revisit their prediction from the beginning of class, to explain why it was correct or incorrect, and to write down what they have learned from class that day. You can find a number of variations on closing questions for a class in *Classroom*

Assessment Techniques (Angelo & Cross, 1993) and by using that phrase to search for other strategies online.

Two other quick points are worth noting here. First, make sure that closing-question activities are processed in some way. Processing opening class predictions or retrievals will come naturally enough, since you have the whole class period in front of you and they will be sitting and waiting expectantly to find out whether they got it right. This can prove more logistically challenging when you ask them to retrieve information or solve problems or exercise skills at the conclusion of class, and they walk out afterward. You can handle this in a few different ways. If it's a simple enough question you have posed at the end, you can make the exercises the penultimate activity and a brief review of the answer the ultimate activity. If you are using a virtual learning environment or social media sites like Twitter or Facebook as a part of your course, you can post the answers there after class. If neither of these options is available, make sure you address the question from the end of the previous class at the beginning of the next class. As we shall see in the next chapter, wrong answers made on activities like this will not necessarily harm student learning as long as they are not allowed to persist uncorrected. Ensure that this does not happen by finding ways to address their responses as soon as possible after the exercise.

Finally, if you do ask students retrieval-based questions either at the beginning or end of the class, you will have to spend at least the first few classes reminding them not to look in their notebooks or their textbooks for the answers. I promise you that this will be their first inclination. Throw out a question about what you have just taught them or about what you did in class last week, and they will immediately begin flipping through their notebooks to find the answer. You will have to remind them that you are not conducting a scavenger hunt for answers or a race to see who can find the answer most quickly. You are helping them remember information, and this will benefit them only if they take the time to draw the information from their brains and not their notebooks. If you spend a lot of time reading about experiments in learning and memory, as I have done while preparing and writing this book, you will notice that almost every experiment uses a control condition in which students simply review their notebooks, textbooks, or key concepts in a study guide. In almost every experiment that I have encountered in this research, *this method proves less effective for long-term retention*. In other words, almost anything that students do with learned information or ideas or skills works more effectively than just looking at your notes about it, even doing so multiple times (although activities such as comparing or rewriting one's notes can produce more positive results). You might want to explain to your students the purpose of opening and closing questions and how it will help them learn the material more deeply; then they won't be so baffled when you introduce small teaching activities that require them to close their books and notebooks and ask them to remember something they have learned, either at the opening or closing of class.

Online Retrieval

The challenge with implementing retrieval practice in online environments is that students are typically working away from you, so you cannot control whether or not they have access to the materials they are tasked with remembering. So while you might be asking them to remember something, they could be just searching for the answers in their notebooks, which will not give them that valuable retrieval practice. With that said, still consider Miller's (2014) suggestions for small teaching activities or course design tweaks as ways to offer students in online or hybrid courses the opportunity to engage in retrieval practice, even if you can't ensure total compliance.

Reading Checks Retrieval practice can begin when students first engage with course materials that you have put online. Include retrieval type questions at the end of every page or section's worth of material, and ensure that students can't get to the next section until they take a brief quiz. Miller pointed to a study in which students who read new material and were quizzed on it in this fashion outperformed nonquizzed students on the final exam. She noted a bonus effect demonstrated by the study: "although the frequent quiz breaks kept students more attentive, they did not seem to tip them over into anxiety; students who did the interspersed quizzes actually reported *less* anxiety about the cumulative test" (p. 78).

Frequent Quizzing Create or find as large of a question bank as possible and require students to take online quizzes frequently. If the bank is large enough, you can allow multiple retakes of the quiz, which would help boost memory because each retake will constitute another instance of retrieval practice. (If the bank is not large enough, you can run into problems with cheating.) As the experiment with the art history lectures demonstrated, and as Miller noted as well, "Short-answer questions do produce a moderate advantage over multiple choice" (p. 108). However, as she also noted, "The best quiz is the one that students will actually *do*—so don't let the perfect be the enemy of the good as you work to create more frequent testing opportunities" (p. 108). If multiple-choice quizzes will ease your grading burden and give you time to create more questions, use multiple-choice questions. Setting time limits on the quiz can help ensure that students don't have a wide-open window to search around in their course materials for answers and might encourage more of them to engage in true retrieval practice on your quizzes.

Space Out Due Dates When you are creating the due dates for your online course, space them out so that quizzes and assessments are occurring on a very regular and frequent schedule (a good practice for face-to-face courses as well, by the way). The more frequently that your students have to check in and offer some demonstration of their learning, the more often you are giving them retrieval practice. Miller recommended setting up "a recurring weekly schedule where each kind of work (discussion, quizzing, homework, any higher-stakes assignments such as major exams or papers) is due on a different day" (p. 109). Such a recommendation will help both with retrieval practice and with interleaving, another key tool for learning.

The Retrieving Syllabus

I'll finish with a simple suggestion for the use of the syllabus to promote retrieval practice. One of the benefits that a syllabus can provide to students is helping them see the overview of the course topics and how they fit together. For this reason I advocate filling out the course schedule section of your syllabus with as much detail as possible. Include phrases or even sentences that describe what will happen in the different units of the course so that students can keep the syllabus as a living document that guides them throughout the semester. If you do this, you can also use it as a small teaching retrieval tool. Require the students to bring their syllabus to class every day, and occasionally use those precious opening and closing minutes of class for a very simple exercise. Have your students pull out their syllabus, and then point them to a previous day's content and ask them to spend a few minutes writing down what they remember about it. You can do this informally, by having them do so in their notebooks, or you could do it in the form of a writing exercise that you collect. You could even do it orally. Point to the date, give them a minute to think, and then collectively ask the class to remind you about what key concepts or skills they took away from that class period or that course unit. Too often, the course syllabus makes an appearance on the first day of the semester and then remains buried in a folder for the rest of the course, serving only as a list of due dates or assignments to complete. Use your course syllabus as a means to foster retrieval practice through brief, small teaching moments in individual class sessions.

PRINCIPLES

Retrieval practice will help your students retain foundational material, which they are most likely to encounter in introductory or entry-level courses in your field. Hence when you are considering how to incorporate retrieval into your teaching repertoire, look first to the lower-level classes you are teaching. The following principles can help guide you through the use of the models above or through the creation of alternative retrieval exercises tailored to your courses.

Frequency Matters The first and last implication of all of this research on retrieval practice is very straightforward: the more students practice retrieval, the better they learn. Frequency matters. The easiest way to implement frequent practice is through regular quizzing. That should be your default strategy. Give quizzes at least once a week, and don't hesitate to give them every class. But all of that quizzing can mean lots of grading, especially if you are using short-answer questions. If you don't want to rely exclusively on quizzes, mix quizzing with small teaching questions (either orally or in writing) at the opening or close of class. Whatever strategy or mix of strategies you choose, implement them as frequently as possible given all of the other demands on your time.

Align Practice and Assessments Whatever type of memory tasks you will ask of your students on your high-stakes assessments (such as midterms and exams) should appear in the retrieval practice you use. If you ask students to remember names and dates of key thinkers in your field on your final exam, make sure they are getting practice in remembering those thinkers throughout the semester. If you give multiple-choice final exams, use clicker questions in class to give them practice in multiple-choice retrieval. If you give them essay exams that require some memory mixed in with thinking, give them writing exercises in class in which they have to answer final exam–type questions.

Require Thinking Remember Willingham's axiom that we remember what we think about? Help your students remember by giving them something to think about. Your retrieval practice might sometimes take the form of simple memory exercises—after all, we likely all have certain key facts or basic information that we want students to have mastered. For example, I want students in my British literature survey course to know that Robert Burns is Scottish because his Scottish identity helped influence much of what he wrote. They can't do higher order analysis of a Burns poem on a final exam if they forget that key fact. But rather than asking students to practice remembering his nationality by selecting it from a list, I can ask them short-answer questions that require them to remember that fact and put it to some use: How does the national identity of Robert Burns influence his writing?

SMALL TEACHING QUICK TIPS: RETRIEVING

Memory retrieval works especially well in brief classroom interventions. You can find room for retrieval in almost any class period or learning session, even if it takes only a minute. But my favorite opportunities for retrieval appear in the opening and closing moments of class, or in the form of regular quizzes or writing exercises.

- Give frequent, low-stakes quizzes (at least weekly) to help your students seal up foundational course content; favor short answers or problem solving whenever possible so that students must process or use what they are retrieving.
- Open class periods or online sessions by asking students to remind you of content covered in previous class sessions; allow students time to reflect for a few moments if you do so orally.
- Close class by asking students to write down the most important concept from that day and one question or confusion that still remains in their minds (i.e., the minute paper).
- Close class by having students take a short quiz or answer written questions about the day's material or solve a problem connected to the day's material.
- Use your syllabus to redirect students to previous course content through quizzes or oral questions and discussion.

CONCLUSION

I have heard college and university teachers express reluctance at the use of regular quizzing because they feel like it infantilizes the students or changes the atmosphere of the classroom from one of shared learning and discussion to one of testing and evaluation. I had those exact same feelings about quizzing when I began my teaching career. I just wanted to engage in interesting discussions with my students about literature and not impede our relationship with heavy-handed tactics like quizzing and testing. Dude.

However, I had too many experiences of having interesting discussions about literature with students who had not done the reading (but who were very good at faking their way through discussions) and who remembered nothing of what we had discussed at the end of the semester for that perspective to last very long. So I understand any emotional hesitation you might feel at the prospect of regular retrieval practice in your classroom, but remember that such practice helps your students learn foundational knowledge as effectively as anything else we know. Think about retrieval practice as I have been arguing for it here: as an activity that lends itself perfectly to small teaching and therefore doesn't require you to devote huge amounts time or energy to it. If you consider it in that light and push yourself to implement regular quizzing or retrieval practice, you will likely find that your students are grateful for it by the end of the semester. In addition to the memory practice it provides them, it also ensures that they stay on top of the reading or homework, which means they won't find themselves stuck at the end of the semester with lots of catching up to do. As always, you can help them recognize the value of those quizzes by teaching transparently. Tell them what the research says about the value of quizzing and retrieval practice and about your decision to use it. They still might not love taking quizzes during the long slogging weeks of October, but they will recognize their value and reap the rewards on those final assessments in December.

Chapter 2

Predicting

INTRODUCTION

Every Thursday night a small group of folks from my college gathers at a local tavern to decompress and socialize. Three of us count ourselves as fans of college football, which means that from September to December we have the added pleasure of keeping our eyes on a football game while we chat. A couple of years ago we decided to liven up our viewing of these games—and other games we might happen to catch over the course of our weekends—by selecting three games each week and making predictions about the winners. We added some modest stakes to this enterprise to make it more interesting: if I predict the most number of games correctly in any given week, the other two each have to buy me a beer the next Thursday. In this particular bar's beer-money exchange rate, that means that I stand to win about $9.00 worth of beer or lose $4.50 per week. Despite this very small prize purse, our little prediction pool has unquestionably ratcheted up our interest in following the games on television. When a close game happens on a Thursday evening, the three of us watch it intently, each emotionally invested in seeing whether our team will win even though the stakes are so low. At times we have tested the patience of the bartenders by sticking around for the final minute of a game to see whether one unranked team beat another in a meaningless September contest.

The stakes of our little pool are raised during the final weeks of the calendar year, when college bowl season arrives and all of the most successful teams from that year are playing in high-profile games against one another and competing for spots in the college football championship games. Our prediction pool continues right to the end, and we each take turns picking the winners in the bowl games, again for a very small prize purse. Successfully predicting the outcome of the end-of-season bowl games requires knowing or remembering a little bit about what happened to each team over the course of the season: How many games did they win or lose? Did they win or lose games against major opponents? Against other bowl teams? Did they perform better or worse than they were expected to perform? Acknowledging the obvious fact that such information doesn't guarantee perfect predictions, the more I can remember about the games that occurred throughout the season, the more informed I will be in predicting the end-of-season bowl games. At the end of the first season in which we played these informal prediction games with one another, while I was looking at the bowl matchups and trying to call to mind whatever I could remember about wins and losses throughout the season, I noticed something striking: the games and teams about which I had the strongest and clearest memories were the ones about which I had made predictions earlier in the season. Over the course of a college football season I might watch several dozen football games, most of which slide from my memory soon afterward. But the games that had featured into our previous prediction exercises stayed with me more firmly than those I had simply watched without having made any kind of guess as to the outcome.

This experience I had with predicting the outcome of games and remembering the actual outcomes afterward more firmly than I remembered games about which I had not made predictions reflects a basic principle that memory researchers have been exploring for many years now: *making predictions about material that you wish to learn increases your ability to understand that material and retrieve it later.* If you had asked me prior to doing any research on this subject how I would have explained the predictive power of my college football experience, I might have offered two folk theories about it. First, making the prediction causes me to pay closer attention to the games than I otherwise might because I am curious to see whether my prediction was correct. I'm more likely to sit and actually watch a game that I have predicted, even a meaningless one in the big picture of the season, than I am to watch a nonpredicted game, which I might be watching while I check my e-mail, read the newspaper, or fold laundry. The simple act of paying close attention might improve my memory of the games. Second, the prediction hooks my emotions into the game. Since I make predictions out of what I believe is my knowledge of college football, each predicted game gives me a little emotional boost of pleasure when I am proven correct and a little sigh of frustration when incorrect. As Chapter 7 will discuss, emotions have the power to focus our attention and give us a quick cognitive boost, so perhaps the tiny emotional investment I make into a predicted game helps lodge it more firmly in my memory.

Although these explanations certainly carry some truth, the power of prediction to improve learning extends beyond attention and emotion and Thursday nights at Joey's Bar and Grill. It offers us a very simple means of helping students acquire both knowledge and comprehension, and it can do so in ways that fit ideally within the realm of small teaching.

IN THEORY

To better understand how and why prediction improves retention and comprehension of learned material, consider first an elegant series of experiments in learning and prediction conducted by three researchers at UCLA and subsequently described in an article in the *Journal of Experimental Psychology: Learning, Memory, and Cognition* (Kornell, Jenson Hayes, and Bjork 2009). The authors asked subjects in one of these experiments to memorize a series of loosely connected word pairs, such as *whale–mammal*. One group of the subjects was given 13 seconds to study each word pair; the other group was given 8 seconds to see only the first word and to make a prediction about the second, after which they had 5 seconds to see the full word pair. Since the two words of the pair did not share obvious connections (since you might well guess *sea* or *ocean* or *large* if you saw only the word *whale*), participants typically guessed the second half of the pair incorrectly. Note also that the subjects in the second (prediction) group had only 5 seconds to view the correct answer, so 8 seconds less than those in the first (nonprediction) group. Yet in spite of this shorter study time, and in spite of the fact that subjects in the second group frequently predicted the second half of the word pair incorrectly, the subjects in the second group performed significantly better than those in the first group when they were asked to recollect the word pairs on a subsequent exam: 67% accuracy in the second group versus 55% in the first. "Unsuccessful retrieval attempts," wrote the authors (by which they mean incorrect predictions of the second half of the word pair), "were, remarkably, more effective than was spending the same time studying the answer to be recalled later" (p. 994). In other words, taking a few seconds to predict the answer before learning it, *even when the prediction is incorrect*, seemed to increase subsequent retention of learned material. This was true even when that prediction time substitutes for—rather than supplements—more conventional forms of studying.

The results of experiments like this one prompted another group of researchers, led by cognitive psychologist Elizabeth Bjork, to see whether they could reproduce this positive learning effect of prediction in an actual classroom (Carey 2014b).

The researchers gave students in Bjork's introductory psychology class short multiple-choice pretests before some of the lectures in her course. Since the questions asked them about material that had not yet been covered, the students performed about as well on the pretests as they would have from guessing randomly—so, again as in the laboratory experiment, they made plenty of wrong guesses. Lectures on the subject matter followed immediately after the pretests, so the students received quick feedback on their answers. At the end of the term, the students took a final exam that contained multiple-choice questions similar to the ones on the pretests. The results paralleled the results of the laboratory experiment almost exactly: students performed around 10% better on questions from the subject areas in which they had been pretested than on those on which they had not. Bjork concluded from this experiment that "giving students a pretest on topics to be covered in a lecture improves their ability to answer related questions about those topics on a later final exam" (Carey 2014b). Note, of course, that even though the vocabulary has changed slightly here—from *prediction* to *pretesting*—the cognitive activity is similar: asking learners to give answers to questions or anticipate outcomes about which they do not yet have sufficient information or understanding.

Before we explore the reasons that prediction boosts learning, consider one final example of prediction in higher education, this one from an online environment (Ogan, Aleven, and Jones 2009). Three researchers from Carnegie Mellon University developed an online tutoring program that demonstrated the power of predicting in helping students improve their intercultural understanding in hybrid language courses. The two French courses described in the experiment each met once a week in a face-to-face environment, but otherwise the students did their course work online. Part of the goal for these courses was to help students develop what the authors called "intercultural competence, that is, the ability to think and act in culturally appropriate ways" (p. 268). This can be an extremely difficult skill to develop, as anyone who has ever traveled in a foreign country can likely attest. The ability to speak the language of a foreign country does not necessarily guarantee your ability to understand how to pay for a cab, order from a menu, or ask a stranger in the Paris Metro which train will take you to the airport in time to catch your flight home (as I once discovered, to my great sorrow). So in this experiment we are moving beyond the realm of simply knowing and retaining information into the broader realm of comprehension—that is, understanding how to use and apply in other contexts the information you have learned. The intercultural competence sought by these instructors requires learners to think and act with their knowledge, not just report it back.

To help students acquire this type of deeper comprehension, two experts in computer-assisted learning worked with a language professor to develop an online tutoring program based on the use of film clips. In the control condition of this experiment, students were shown film clips highlighting *cultural attitudes or behaviors* (270) that are normally taught in introductory French classes. As the students watched the short film clips, they had the opportunity to take notes on what they saw. The students in the experimental group, by contrast, were given the opportunity to use the power of prediction to improve their learning. Their film clips would pause at key moments, ask them to make a prediction about what was about to unfold, and then require them to ponder what actually happened once the clip had finished: the authors described their three-part sequence with the catchy phrase *pause–predict–ponder*. The prediction the students had to make actually came from a drop-down menu of choices, but then they had open text boxes to explain why they made that prediction. After they had watched the remainder of the clip, they had to answer a simple question about whether or not their prediction was correct and then respond to prompts to help them reflect on their prediction, such as: "If so [i.e., if your prediction was correct], did you see anything you didn't expect about the French culture? If not, what happened that you didn't predict?" Students in both conditions concluded their viewing of the film clips with required postings to a discussion board to allow them to process and review what they had seen.

After the class the researchers looked at two different measures to see whether the pause–predict–ponder exercises had improved student mastery of intercultural competence: student scores on tests of cultural knowledge, and their more general cultural thinking or reasoning skills through their discussion board posts. The students who had the opportunity to make predictions outscored their peers on the first exam by about that same 10% margin that we saw in the earlier experiments, with some diminishing returns on the subsequent assignments—which might tell us that prediction, like many of the active learning interventions in this book, especially helps new learners. Ratings of the posts in the discussion board also showed the students in the experimental condition performing significantly higher on assessments of intercultural competence than those in the control condition. In the discussion of their results, the researchers noted that students made correct predictions only about 40% of the time, another point in favor of the notion (to be qualified shortly) that wrong predictions do no harm. They also pointed to an interesting side benefit they witnessed: students in the experimental condition posted more frequently on the discussion boards, and more frequently on target, than those in the control condition. "The experimental group showed a better ability to maintain a productive discussion compared to the control group (p. 283)." It seems that in this case the prediction activity also helped engage the students more thoroughly in the material, just as it did with my Thursday night football games.

To better understand how prediction both aids retention (or the memorization of facts) and comprehension (or the use of those facts in other contexts), it helps to understand briefly a topic to which we will return in Chapter 5: the connected nature of knowledge. As Benedict Carey put it in *How We Learn*, "The brain does not store facts, ideas, and experiences like a computer does, as a file that is clicked open, always displaying the identical image. It embeds them in networks of perceptions, facts, and thoughts" (Carey 2014a p. 20). An easy way to illustrate this notion of networked knowledge is to point to the difference between an expert in a subject (such as you) and a novice learner (such as your student). When your student encounters facts in your discipline for the first time, she picks them up as fragmented, isolated units, almost like dates of historical events scattered randomly across a timeline. If I pointed to any one of those dates, a novice learner who has memorized the facts could tell me a single thing about it: 1865, End of the American Civil War. But now imagine that I pointed to this date and asked an American historian to tell me about it. He would have a huge network of other information he could provide to me about that date, and he could also connect that date to other relevant dates on the timeline. That date links in his mind to dozens or hundreds of other facts. And that, according to one basic understanding of human knowing, is what constitutes knowledge: the web of connections we have between the things we know. According to *How Learning Works: Seven Research-Based Principles for Smart Teaching*, an important difference between the knowledge of experts and novices is "the number or density of connections among the concepts, facts, and skills they know" (Ambrose, Bridges, DiPietro, Lovett, and Norman 2010, p. 49). Experts have dense weaves of connections between all of the facts and information they know, and novices have sparse and incomplete ones. Density of connections affects both knowledge and comprehension. When new facts are woven into a dense network of connections, they are implanted there more firmly and are more likely to be activated in multiple contexts. And because they are tied to lots of other facts and information, the expert can more easily see how to use and apply a fact in other contexts than a novice.

We will dig more into this theory of knowledge in Chapter 4, but for now you have enough information to understand one major reason that prediction helps learners retain and use new information: predictive activities prepare your mind for learning by driving you to seek connections that will help you make an accurate prediction. Carey (2014b) explains it like this:

> [Predictive activities] reshape our mental networks by embedding unfamiliar concepts … into questions we at least partly comprehend … Even if the question is not entirely clear and its solution unknown, a guess will in itself begin to link the questions to possible answers. And those networks light up like Christmas lights when we hear the concepts again.

In other words, when you are forced to make a prediction or give an answer to a question about which you do not have sufficient information, you are compelled to search around for *any* possible information you might have that could relate to the subject matter and help you make a plausible prediction. That search activates prior knowledge you have about the subject matter and prepares your brain to slot the answer, when you receive it, into a more richly connected network of facts. Prediction helps lay a foundation for richer, more connected knowing. Roediger and his coauthors in *Make It Stick* describe it this way: "Unsuccessful attempts to solve a problem encourage deep processing of the answer when it is later supplied, creating fertile ground for its encoding, in a way that simply reading the answer cannot"

(Brown, Roediger, and McDaniel 2014, p. 88). The ground is fertile because the learner's brain has now activated several connections between the question and other possible contexts, and when the answer arrives in the soil it takes hold more quickly and firmly because of the link between the answer and those other contexts.

This seems to be the main virtue of predictive activities in terms of the mechanics of cognition. But Carey (2014b) offered two other possible explanations for why prediction activities may help with learning. First, when students are asked to make predictions or given pretests on course material, in the ways that happened in Bjork's experiment, they have a clearer understanding of what their final assessment might look like—and that, in turn, might improve their subsequent study activities and preparation strategies. As Bjork pointed out, "Taking a practice test and getting answers wrong seems to improve subsequent study, because the test adjusts our thinking in some way to the kind of material we need to know" (Carey 2014b). Pretests or predictive activities alert the students to what the teacher sees as important for them to know and direct their study to those areas. To take a simple example, three courses in my department provide surveys of large areas of British or American literature. They are all taught by different professors, one of whom is me. At least one of my colleagues believes it important that students know names of the major authors and dates and titles of their major works, and he tests them on that information in his exams. I don't view that information as a priority in my survey and instead focus my exams on the ability of students to recognize broader historical and literary trends in the period. A student who moves from my colleague's survey course to mine might spend the first half of my course, until the midterm exam, intent on remembering names and dates and titles. She wouldn't know that although that information might prove useful on my essay exams, her real task is to recognize broad historical trends and make connections. A quick pretest in my course would help her recognize how to modify her study strategies in my class to succeed on my exams, and not the exams she might envision I would give based on the last survey class she took. Even informal predictive activities that I might use in the classroom, like asking students to speculate on how a historical event might influence subsequent literary developments, will help establish for them the focus areas of the course.

Second, prediction activities might help us recognize more accurately the gaps in our knowledge. "Wrong guesses," Carey wrote, "expose our fluency illusions, our false impression that we 'know' the capital of Eritrea because we just saw it or once studied it…. Pretesting operates as a sort of fluency vaccine" (Carey 2014b). Illusions of fluency represent one of the foremost challenges we face in helping students learn subject matter deeply. Anyone who has taught for more than a year or two has encountered the befuddled student who comes to office hours after an exam or assignment and explains that he studied the material for many hours and thought he had it down cold. Such a student is laboring under the illusion of fluency, possibly because he engaged in common study strategies like reading the textbook or reviewing his notes over and over again. The literature on human learning repeatedly reveals, however, that those strategies prove effective primarily for short-term learning. If we want long-term learning from our students, we have to teach them (and advise them to study for themselves) with more active learning strategies like the ones described in these chapters. Students who take pretests or make predictions are forced to confront the depth of their knowledge, and that confrontation—when it reveals gaps or weaknesses—might spur them to better or more determined learning.

We have to qualify the claim I made earlier in this chapter that wrong predictions do not seem to harm future learning: Learners do have to receive fairly immediate feedback on the accuracy of their predictions or pretest answers if we don't want those wrong answers to leave a deeper impression than the correct ones. In all of the aforementioned experiments, the learners were given that immediate feedback: in the case of the first experiment, it came within 8 seconds; in the language tutorial, the film continued immediately after students wrote their explanation, which helps explain why the wrong answers they originally gave did not stick. No doubt wrong answers can stick or lead to confusion if they are left uncorrected. So although prediction activities must have quick follow-up responses, I have seen no specific formula for how immediately the feedback has to arrive. It seems likely that the sooner it arrives the better—if not in the same class session as the prediction activity, then at least by the next class period.

There is one final point to be made before we explore some models of how instructors can use prediction activities in their courses. We can think about predictive activities as a cognitive version of something we normally ask of learners who are attempting to master a skill: namely, requiring them to engage that skill before they are prepared to complete it successfully. We can all likely draw from our experiences in remembering attempts to master skills of one sort or another, and we know full well that however much one might read in advance about throwing a football or painting a portrait or giving a speech, the real learning happens after we have thrown ourselves into the situation and made that first (unsuccessful) attempt. When I took a class to become licensed in scuba diving, we spent the first half of every session in a classroom taking notes on some skill we would have to practice in the pool. I typically jumped in the pool for the second half of class thinking I had that skill mastered; within a few minutes my fluency illusions were dispelled, and I floundered around for a while, doing it completely wrong until the instructor swam over and gave me some (immediate) feedback, at which point the real learning began.

We facilitate this type of learning in academic environments all the time, asking students to try out cognitive skills that they have not yet fully developed. I don't spend the entire semester lecturing to my freshman composition students about all of the writing techniques they will need to write a perfect academic essay and then give them one final assignment to show me how they have mastered those skills. I assign essays from the beginning of the semester, even though some of what they need to write great academic essays won't be covered for another 4 or 8 or 12 weeks. Asking students to make predictions before learning new material just represents another version of this common teaching approach.

MODELS

The ideal grounds for small teaching activities related to prediction are the same ones that can prove so effective for retrieval: the opening and closing minutes of class periods. The opening minutes of a class might include the opportunity for students to make predictions about what will be covered in that class period; prediction activities in the final minutes of class will help prepare them for the work they will be completing prior to the next class session. Consider the following models for leveraging those opening and closing minutes of class for prediction activities.

Pretesting

For both retention and comprehension, you can follow the lead of Elizabeth Bjork and her colleagues by giving your students pretests on course material they are about to learn. You could do this in an endless variety of ways: a major pretest at the beginning of the semester, equivalent to the final exam; smaller pretests prior to each unit of the course; or even very brief pretests prior to that day's lecture class. The small teaching approach would seem to point toward the direction of those quick daily (or perhaps weekly) pretests as the least disruptive to a normal schedule and as the easiest to incorporate into a normal teaching routine. If you want to help direct students toward the type of learning that will serve them well on the major assessments for the course, the same question format should be used for both pretests and full-length assessments. So if you normally give a final exam with multiple-choice questions, give multiple-choice pretests. If you normally ask essay questions, ask an essay question—but perhaps one that can be answered with a short response instead of a long essay. You don't have to grade the pretests individually, but you should give immediate feedback on them. You can review the answers with the entire class immediately after the pretest is completed and have students check their own work. It should go without saying that pretests are not graded, but you could certainly collect them and use them to take attendance or to get a handle on the prior knowledge of your students in a given subject area. You could even do the pretesting orally, in a discussion format, by throwing out the question and allowing 5 minutes for students to give responses.

In all cases of pretesting, you should make absolutely clear to the students the purpose of what you are doing so that they don't feel as if you are unfairly asking them about material they haven't learned yet. Talk to them about the power of prediction and be transparent in your use of it, especially in activities that might look or feel like graded assessments.

Clicker Predictions

Clickers present a very simple route to prediction questions, as Derek Bruff pointed out in his book *Teaching With Classroom*

Response Systems: Creating Active Learning Environments (Bruff 2009). His chapter "A Taxonomy of Clicker Questions" categorizes prediction questions as a form of question that asks students to apply knowledge, which points to the power of prediction to increase comprehension in addition to the benefits it should provide in boosting memory of individual facts and concepts. For example, Bruff gave an example of a math instructor at a small college who "shows his students a graphing program that allows him to vary a parameter in a function, such as the parameter ω in the function $\sin(\omega t)$, and asks his students to predict what will happen to the graph of a function when he changes that parameter. After the students vote with their clickers, he demonstrates the correct answer using his graphing program" (p. 85). Students cannot answer questions like this with simple plug-and-chug–type knowledge; they have to possess a conceptual understanding of the problem to make an accurate prediction. They have to *reason with* a formula rather than just *repeat* a formula.

Bruff also noted that clickers can support the opportunity for instructors to ask students for predictions behind the screen of anonymity, which can be useful in certain contexts. He provided an example of a health and wellness course at another university in which instructors want to draw attention to student perceptions of drinking on campus. The instructors first ask the students how many alcoholic drinks they consumed at their last social occasion, but then they also ask students to predict what they think the responses of their peers will look like. "The differences between the predicted votes and the actual votes," explained Bruff, "are often surprising to students because it turns out that students are not always as risky as they think they are" (p. 86). The benefit of such a quick prediction exercise is the rich discussion that follows: "This activity can lead to a productive classwide discussion of social perceptions of risky behavior and the role that marketing, in particular, plays in those perceptions" (p. 86). Such discussions, in other words, can encourage the students to reflect on why their predictions were incorrect—and the role that social media or beer commercials might play in driving their perceptions of their peers' consumption of alcohol. The potential screen of anonymity provided by clickers obviously can serve a useful purpose when asking students to make predictions based on their own personal behaviors. It also could prove useful anytime you feel students might not want their predictions shared publicly, either because they want something kept private or because they feel they might be embarrassed by making a wildly incorrect prediction in front of their peers (or in front of you).

Prediction–Exposure–Feedback

Even without formal testing or the use of clickers, you can always ask students to make informal, in-class predictions about any course material to which they are about to be exposed. This could happen in almost any discipline, in any type of class. Scientists know full well how prediction plays a role in the scientific method—in the form of the hypothesis—and likely already ask students to engage in predictive activities in their use of laboratory experiments and reports. But outside of the laboratory, and in other disciplines, instructors can still follow this same basic approach. If students have done some advanced reading from the textbook, which you plan to cover in more depth in lecture that day, you might begin that lecture by asking them to apply some concept they read about in the textbook to an example with which you will begin the day's class session. If their reading covered a specific economic theory, for example, you might open class by describing a specific historical context and asking them to explain what that economic theory would predict will happen in that context. Or you can always ask students to make predictions about new content based on their knowledge from earlier in the semester, from their previous courses, or from their own general knowledge. *How Learning Works* gave two quick examples of this: "Before asking students to read an article from the 1970s, you might ask them what was going on historically at the time that might have informed the author's perspective. Or when presenting students with a design problem, you might ask them how a famous designer, whose work they know, might have approached the problem." In these kinds of questions, again, you are requiring students "not only to draw on prior knowledge but also to use it to reason about new knowledge" (Ambrose, Bridges, DiPietro, Lovett, and Norman 2010, p. 33). Ideally, you will both ask for the prediction and give them the opportunity to explain why they made it; doing so will require them to examine their thinking and might help them recognize fluency illusions. Even more ideally, after you give them the answer you might ask them to explain why their predictions did or did not hold true.

To offer one final example, when I teach novels in my literature courses we frequently have to spread the reading of a single novel over the course of multiple class periods. Asking students at the end of one of the intermediate sessions to make a prediction about what will happen in the reading for the next class period, as I sometimes like to do, requires them to reflect on what they know about the novel's characters to predict what they might do next; it also inspires them to think about what plot strategies they have encountered thus far and whether those strategies will continue. Does this author create only events that stem very organically from previous events, or does this author like to drop surprises on his characters out of the blue? Prediction, in other words, forces them to marshal what they know thus far about the novel to anticipate what comes next. Of course, any discipline that lends itself to narrative exposition, such as history, could create pauses at any moment in the narrative—just as I might do with the novels I am teaching—and ask students to predict what comes next. Even disciplines that are not explicitly driven by narrative likely have narrative moments, in the form of key historical developments in the discipline or famous experiments, all of which would lend themselves to prediction and subsequent content exposure.

Closing Predictions

Predictions can close a class as easily as they can open them, but in the case of closing predictions you are pointing students toward the material that they will be reading or studying for homework. Many textbooks include prediction questions at the beginning of a chapter; I suspect that few students read or think about those questions unless they are specifically required to do so. You might spend 5 minutes at the end of a class raising one of those questions and asking students to respond to it either orally or in writing. A 5-minute effort to answer a question about the coming material based on the material from the previous chapter or lecture should provide a small boost of interest and attention as students head off to complete the nightly homework. Obviously you don't need textbook questions to accomplish this goal; you can devise your own questions that will require them to make predictions about homework material. You can push this activity one step further by asking students to revisit the question in the opening minutes of the next class and reflect on whether or not they got it right and why they did (or didn't). This would push them into a deeper place of analyzing their own state of understanding and observing how it evolved while they were doing the homework. To continue with the previous example, I might close my class by asking students how they think the novel will end and then collecting their responses. At the beginning of the next class, I could return those responses to them and ask them to tell me what really happened at the end of the novel and why they got it right—or wrong.

PRINCIPLES

Asking students to make predictions requires a very small investment of time, which makes predicting an ideal small teaching activity. The following principles can help guide the creation of prediction activities in your classroom.

Stay Conceptual Remember that part of the reason predictions work is that they require students to draw up whatever knowledge they might have that will assist them in making their prediction. If you ask them questions that are so specific that they have no prior knowledge to activate, you won't see this benefit. It seems unlikely, for example, that asking students to predict the meaning of a word in a language with which they are totally unfamiliar, in a different alphabet, will offer much learning benefit. Focus prediction activities on the major conceptual material that will maximize their learning in the course.

Provide Fast Feedback Close the loop on every prediction your students make by providing feedback as immediately as possible. Predictions made at the opening of a class session should be addressed within that class session. Those made at the end, even if they should be answered by the reading or studying they will do for the next session, should still be reviewed at the opening of that next session. Predictions made in online environments should provide feedback within the same session they are made. Remember that you don't want wrong predictions hanging around in students' heads for very long; the more immediate the correction, the better.

Induce Reflection As Daniel Willingham argued, "Memory is the residue of thought" (p. 54). In other words, we remember what we spend a little time thinking about. Prediction provides an excellent spur for thought, in that you can ask students to think about why they made their prediction, what actually happened (if the prediction leads to direct observation), and why their prediction was right or wrong. If you are asking students at the beginning of a class to write down a prediction and having a few of them read their predictions aloud, return to those students at the end of class and ask them to explain why they made those predictions. Students who made correct predictions can be asked to articulate the principle or concept that helped them get it right; students who made incorrect predictions can repair their understanding by articulating the correct ideas.

SMALL TEACHING QUICK TIPS: PREDICTING

With prediction we move beyond the foundational act of memorization into more complex cognitive territories. But that doesn't mean you can't still make use of quick strategies and brief windows of time to incorporate prediction into your courses. These reliable prediction activities give you some easy starting points.

- At the beginning of the class, unit, or course, give students a brief pretest on the material. For example, give an opening-week pretest that is similar in format to the final exam.
- Prior to first content exposure, ask students to write down what they already know about that subject matter or to speculate about what they will be learning.
- When presenting cases, problems, examples, or histories, stop before the conclusion and ask students to predict the outcome.
- When you are teaching a new cognitive skill (e.g., writing in a new genre), let students try their hand at it (and receive feedback) before they feel ready.
- Close class by asking students to make predictions about material that will be covered in the next class session.

CONCLUSION

In the introduction to this chapter I noted that my own initial folk theories about my college football experience would have focused on attention and emotion: making a prediction nudges me to pay closer attention to what happens, and it draws me into the game emotionally. In this chapter we considered the mechanics of learning and prediction from a more cognitive perspective, but we shouldn't discount the role that attention and emotion play in this process. Predictions make us curious—I wonder whether I will be right?—and curiosity is an emotion that has been recently demonstrated to boost memory when it is heightened prior to exposure to new material. A recent report in *Scientific American* described an experiment in which research subjects were given questions, asked to rate how curious those questions made them, and then exposed to both an unrelated object (an image of a face) and the answer. The subjects afterward were tested on their ability to remember both the faces and the answers, and the researchers found that the more curious the subjects were about the question, the more likely they were to remember both the faces and the answers. This (curious) result suggests that heightening our curiosity not only makes us interested in the answer to the question but also just generally stimulates our brain to pay closer attention and remember what it encounters. "The researchers found," the article notes, "that curious minds showed increased activity in the hippocampus, which is involved in the creation of memories." Further, the anticipation of receiving an answer to a question about which the subjects were curious stimulated the reward system of the brain, and that system in turn stimulated the hippocampus further: "The brain's reward system seemed to prepare the hippocampus for learning." Curiosity and anticipation of an answer, taken together, led the brains of these subjects to snap to attention and form deeper and longer memories (Yuhas 2014).

Asking someone to make a prediction represents a very simple route to raising curiosity and hence represents a very simple route to stimulating the brains of our students and preparing them for their learning. When we make a prediction, we want to know whether we were right or not—whether we are predicting the winner of a football game, the ending of a novel, the next move of a character in a video, or the outcome of a science experiment. Consider how you can use the opening or closing minutes of your class or brief questions seeded throughout a lesson to till the soil of your students' minds and prepare a fertile ground for the learning that will follow.

Chapter 3

Interleaving

INTRODUCTION

One of the sabbatical projects I undertook while writing this book was learning Spanish, a task I had attempted but then abandoned during graduate school many years ago. Although ostensibly I embarked upon this more recent endeavor in preparation for some upcoming travel to Latin America, in truth I count studying and learning languages as one of my favorite pastimes. (I will pause here to allow you to savor the fact that you probably lead a more socially engaging life than I do.) My school language learning includes Latin, Greek, and French, but I have also made independent efforts to learn Spanish, Italian, and Gaelic at various points in my life. I wouldn't get very far conversing with the residents of ancient Rome or the native Gaelic speakers of Ireland's Aran Islands, but some aspects of all of those languages have stayed with me. Because I have spent so many hours memorizing foreign language vocabulary and studying grammatical structures of other languages, the process has become one with which I am comfortable and familiar. Even though it had been a few years since I launched a full and earnest effort to master a language, I assumed that my Spanish study would come easily enough as long as I put in the requisite time and effort.

My course of study began with an online program that I hoped would guide me through the early stages of review and basic acquisition, after which I would expand to other activities like reading novels or watching television shows in Spanish. For a month or two, I spent 15 minutes every day online listening to brief sentences in Spanish, repeating them back into the computer microphone, translating Spanish sentences into English and vice versa, and taking occasional quizzes. The individual lessons of the program were broken into segments that took about five minutes to complete, which meant I could complete three new ones every day. Each new segment included a small measure of reinforcement of the material I had already learned, but the lessons focused mostly on acquiring new vocabulary or identifying new rules of grammar or syntax. A month into following this schedule of three new lessons per day, I found myself increasingly forgetting vocabulary I had learned just days before and regularly failing the occasional timed quizzes I took. I would learn the word for "tie" (*corbata*), and then the next day mix it up with the word for "belt" (*cinturon*). A few weeks later, one of those words would pop up for review, and I wouldn't remember either of them. My progress in understanding the language seemed very slow in contrast to my previous experiences. Every lesson felt like a new struggle to me. I assumed that the program—which multiple people had recommended to me—had been constructed by folks who knew something about language acquisition and that therefore the problem must lie with me. Either I was not spending enough time on my study, or my aging brain was no longer as adept as it once was in learning languages. All I could think to do was redouble my time and effort.

Then one day I noticed a tab on the home page labeled Strengthen Skills. I clicked on it, and it took me through a 5-minute review session that mimicked the activities of the normal lessons but introduced nothing new and contained only vocabulary and sentence structures that I had already covered. At first I found it frustrating to complete these exercises since I was stumbling over vocabulary that I had supposedly learned already, but I began gradually incorporating more and more of these review sessions into my learning time. Eventually my routine shifted from three new lessons per day to one new lesson per day and two review sessions. Within weeks of making this change I felt the budding mastery that had been eluding me begin to emerge; I began regularly acing the timed quizzes and feeling much more comfortable with my pronunciation efforts. Of course, my progress through new material slowed down, but this seemed like a small price to pay for a much more firm understanding of that new material through these repeated review sessions. Perhaps most important, what had felt like a painful struggle to me now became enjoyable.

IN THEORY

The learning principle that helps explain this improvement in my language acquisition skills is called interleaving, and it involves two related activities that promote high levels of long-term retention: (a) spacing out learning sessions over time; and (b) mixing up your practice of skills you are seeking to develop. A study conducted almost 30 years ago on French language acquisition in an American high school provides our first illustration of this principle (Bloom and Shuell 1981). The researchers divided around 50 students into two groups and charged each group with learning 20 new French vocabulary words in different ways. The first group had a single 30-minute session in which they studied the new vocabulary words and completed three separate tasks on them, such as filling in the French word after receiving the English equivalent. The second group had the exact same length of study time and the exact same set of written exercises, but they were separated into three 10-minute study periods over the course of 3 consecutive days. The contrast between these two methods is usually described in the literature as *massed* versus *spaced* (or sometimes *distributed*) learning. In massed learning, students focus entirely on one skill or set of material until they have mastered it; in distributed practice, students space out their learning sessions over time. At the end of the study periods for both groups in this experiment, the students were given a vocabulary test on the words; both groups averaged about 16 of 20 words correct. This finding will appear again and again in the literature; for short-term retention, massed practice can be as effective (and sometimes more effective) than distributed practice. The researchers then returned to the classroom a week later, without any prior warning to the students, and tested them on the vocabulary again. This time the results diverged sharply: the massed practice students remembered around 11 of the vocabulary words, whereas the spaced practice students remembered around 15. Remember that both groups had the same total learning time and completed the same tasks; only the spacing of their learning activities differed.

A substantial body of research has demonstrated the power of spaced learning. Benedict Carey wrote in *How We Learn* that "nothing in learning science comes close in terms of immediate, significant, and reliable improvements to learning" (p. 76). The theory that explains the power of spaced learning stems at least in part from what we have learned about the importance of retrieval practice. One of the challenges to our memories is the ability to pull desired information from our long-term memories when we need it. The more times we practice drawing specific skills or information from our long-term memory, the better we get at it. When we engage in massed learning exercises, focusing on one set of content repeatedly, we never have to access the learned material from the deeper recesses of our long-term memory.

By contrast, if we use spaced learning to allow some time for the forgetting of learned material to set in, we are forced to draw material from our longer-term memory when we return to it. Spacing out learning thus forces us to engage at least partially in memory retrieval.

That forced cycle of forgetting and retrieving is only half the explanation for the power of spaced learning. As the authors of *Make It Stick* explain, the time that intervenes between spaced learning sessions also allows our minds to better organize and solidify what we are studying:

> Embedding new learning in long-term memory requires a process of consolidation, in which memory traces (the brain's representations of new learning) are strengthened, given meaning, and connected to prior knowledge—a process that unfolds over hours and may take several days. Rapid-fire practice leans on short-term memory. Durable learning, however, requires time for mental rehearsal... Hence, spaced practice works better. The increased effort to retrieve the learning after a little forgetting has the effect of retriggering consolidation, further strengthening memory. (Brown, Roediger, and McDaniel 2014, p. 49)

Our brains need time to undertake the processes of encoding, consolidating, and organizing newly learned material, and the gaps between spaced learning sessions allow it that time. If you have ever slogged your way through some difficult learning exercise, left it in frustration, and then—hours or days later—returned to it with a mysteriously firmer grasp of it than you had previously, you have experienced the phenomenon described by the authors of *Make It Stick*. I remember this happening to me time and time again when I played the piano more regularly. I would stand up from a practice session convinced that I would never master some difficult passage and then sit down the next day and find that it had mysteriously become much easier than it was the day before.

The implications of this principle are clear enough for both learners and teachers: we should help students space out their learning both in how we design our courses and in how we encourage them to study. However, we can help our students even further if we consider spaced learning as one aspect of *interleaving*, a broader approach to helping our students learn. Interleaving refers to the practice of spending some time learning one thing and then pausing to concentrate on learning a second thing before having quite mastered that first thing, and then returning to the first thing, and then moving onto a third thing, and then returning to the second thing, and so forth. In short, it involves the process of both spacing and mixing learning activities—the spacing happening by virtue of the mixing. As a simple example, suppose that I want to teach my students four major concepts: A, B, C, and D. Standard educational practice would have us spend 3 weeks on concept A, 3 weeks on concept B, 3 weeks on concept C, and 3 weeks on concept D. I might have a unit test at the end of each 3-week period and then a cumulative final exam. An interleaved approach would look quite different. I might instead spend the first 2 weeks introducing all four concepts, giving students a brief overview of them each. Then for 2 weeks I would dig in on concept A (followed by a quiz) and another 2 weeks on concept B (another quiz). We would pause at that point and review both concepts together and then take an exam. We would repeat the pattern with concepts C and D and then review all four concepts together for a couple of weeks before we would take that final exam. At the end of Week 3 my students are not going to know concept A as well as the students who spent 3 weeks learning it in the standard form. According to all of the research we have on interleaving, though, they are going to know it much better than the students in the massed example at the end of the semester—and, more importantly, after they have left the course.

As you are reading this, you are perhaps thinking to yourself that this all sounds very messy and might even provoke frustration from you and your students since it would be much neater and cleaner to march your way through the concepts in order. Indeed it would, and the research on interleaving confirms what you suspect: learners often find it frustrating. I experienced this frustration myself when I began using that Strengthen Skills tab in my language-learning program and found that I didn't know nearly as much as I thought I did. Research also tells us that massed practice works very effectively for short-term learning, which is why students like it and why they can often perform well on exams when they engage in massed learning exercises like cramming. Jeanette Norden, a neuroscientist who has taught medical students at Vanderbilt University for several decades now using an interleaved approach, compares teaching this way to a form of spiraling. The first time you approach the material, you are making a single spiral at the bottom level. The next time you return to it you are circling back through the material but at a slightly higher level. Spiraling can feel frustrating to the learner because you are, in a sense, going around in circles. However, you are also moving upward with each spiral, adding new layers of learning every time you push back through the material. The effectiveness of Norden's approach to medical education, which has been seen as unconventional by many of her peers, is evident enough in the results. One of the teachers profiled in Ken Bain's book *What the Best College Teachers Do*, Norden has "won every award for teaching granted by the medical school and selected by the students—some of the awards more times than the university will allow" (p. 6). Her students have consistently registered outstanding performances on the neuroscience portion of the national Medical Licensing Exam. Norden's experiences suggest that a little discomfort during the interleaved learning process can have major payoffs in the long run.

Laboratory studies that have been conducted comparing massed versus interleaved learning likewise leave little doubt that interleaving trumps massing for long-term retention by a very wide margin. Consider a frequently cited study in this area in which students were tasked with the challenge of learning to solve math problems involving different geometric shapes (Rohrer and Taylor 2007). In this experiment the students all received brief tutorials on how to calculate the volume of four different geometric shapes, including seeing a worked example, and then were asked to solve 16 different problems that required them to use what they had learned. The tutorials and problem-solving sessions took place on two separate occasions, a week apart. In one group, the Blockers, the students had a tutorial and then solved four problems on it; had a second tutorial and then solved four problems on it; and so on. In the other group, the Mixers, the students received all four tutorials at once and then were given the 16 problems in random order. While the students were working on the problems, the Blockers performed better. During the first learning session, for example, the Blockers solved 89 percent of the problems correctly; the Mixers solved only 60 percent of them correctly. One week after the practice sessions were completed, the groups returned to the laboratory and were given a new set of eight problems, in random order, two on each of the four shapes. The difference between the groups is astonishing: the success rate of the Blockers dropped down to 20 percent, whereas the success rate of the Mixers *improved* to 63 percent.

In this experiment, both groups engaged in spaced learning; they had two distinct sessions, separated by a week, and the test was given a week after that. We don't have a comparison group in which, say, students completed 32 problems in one massed session instead of the two separate sessions spaced a week apart, but we can assume from previous research on massed versus spaced learning that both the Blockers and Mixers would have outperformed that group. So given that both groups engaged in spaced learning, this experiment particularly highlights the benefits of interleaved learning: mixing your study or practice as well as spacing it. The authors of the study present this brief explanation for why they believe the Mixers so definitively outperformed the Blockers: "The superior test performance after mixed practice is, in our view, attributed to the fact that students in this condition were required to know not only *how* to solve each kind of problem but also *which* procedure (i.e., formula) was appropriate for each kind of problem (i.e., solid)" (Rohrer and Taylor 2007, pp. 493–494). In other words, the Mixers had to learn not only how to plug and chug the mathematical equations but also how to identify the *type* of problem they were seeing and to select the formula that would work for that problem. They could not work on autopilot, as a student might do in a class session in which he learns Formula A and then applies it to Problem Type A for an extended period of time, knowing that Formula A will always work for Problem Type A, and every problem he will see in the session will be Problem Type A. Hence, "a significant advantage of interleaving and variation," argued the authors of *Make It Stick*, "is that they help us learn better how to assess context and discriminate between problems, selecting and applying the correct solution from a range of possibilities" (Brown, Roediger, and McDaniel 2014, p. 53). And this is important, as they note, because real-world performance contexts require this skill: in life, as on final exams, "problems and opportunities come at us unpredictably, out of sequence. For our learning to have practical value, we must be adept at discerning 'What kind of problem is this?' so we can select and apply an appropriate solution" (p. 53). Blocked learning does not require students to make such choices about which learned skill to apply in which context.

. This explanation for the limits of blocked practice and the benefits of interleaving points to a deep and fundamental challenge that all learners face: transferring learning from the original context in which we encounter it into novel or unfamiliar contexts. A great deal of research has been done in this area, and the consensus has been that fundamentally we are not very good at doing this. "Transfer," wrote Michelle Miller in *Minds Online*, "is remarkably hard to achieve, a particularly unsettling fact given that it is also such a high-stakes issue; after all, an education that doesn't transfer isn't worth much" (Miller 2014, p. 130). We learn in specific contexts, those concepts become familiar to us, and we have trouble transferring that learning into other contexts. So students who learn a specific writing skill in my composition class never think to apply it to the history paper they are writing; students who master the scientific method in biology don't think to apply it in the psychology course they are taking. Blocked study or practice deepens our association between a learned skill or concept and the specific context in which we learned it; interleaved learning, by contrast, forces us into frequent transfers of information and skills across contexts, which helps us develop the ability to recognize when a learned skill might apply in a new context. The students in the math experiment, when they were taking that final test, were faced with novel problems in random order. The students who had engaged in mixed practice were much more effective than the blockers at rooting around in their memory for the full set of skills they had learned and applying them in this new context. Cultivating the ability of our students to draw from memory and apply learned concepts or skills to new situations is, as Susan Ambrose and her colleagues argued, the "central goal of education" (Ambrose, Bridges, DiPietro, Lovett,

Norman 2010, p. 108). Interleaved learning facilitates that goal more effectively than massed learning.

Before we push into the models for interleaving in higher education pedagogy, though, I have to offer one essential clarification. In the initial learning phase, blocked study or practice is not a bad thing—and for some types of learning tasks it might even be a necessary thing. A recent study by two psychologists at Iowa State University compared the effects of blocked and interleaved practice on students who were learning the pronunciations of French words (Carpenter and Mueller 2013). Over the course of several experiments, they found consistently that the students who had the opportunity to repeat the pronunciation of familiar words over and over again in blocked fashion outperformed those who learned those pronunciations in interleaved fashion. Their survey of the literature also points to one or two experiments in which blocked learners have outperformed interleavers on certain types of tasks (although they acknowledge that the bulk of published studies supports interleaving). The final recommendation they make in their conclusion, though, seems like an eminently sensible one: "Rather than using a schedule that is exclusively blocked or interleaved, it may be more advantageous to start with a blocked schedule and then transition to interleaving" (p. 680). Blocked study or practice, it seems to me, is an appropriate first step for any learning activity. As Benedict Carey put it, "It's not that repetitive [or massed] practice is *bad*. We all need a certain amount of it to become familiar with any new skill or material" (Carey, 2014a, p. 157). Indeed, I suspect most of us introduce new material to our students, or learn it ourselves, by blocking the study or practice of it. We have to begin the learning process by spending some concentrated time or effort on the task. The argument I am making here is not to eliminate blocked practice but to use interleaving to require students to return continuously, in different contexts, to material they have learned already.

Blocking on its own is not a problem; blocking without interleaving—otherwise known as cramming—produces wonderful short-term retention but will leave our students without the long-term retention that will enable them to extend their learning beyond the final exam.

MODELS

The application of the small teaching philosophy to the learning principle of interleaving occurs less in the form of specific in-class activities than in the form of tweaks or modifications to your course design. So the following models focus less on discipline-based examples and more on how to achieve interleaving in three different contexts: (a) through the design of your assessment plan; (b) through the organization of your class time; and (c) through the use of an online course management system.

Cumulative Learning

If you combine the research we have considered on the importance of retrieval practice and the research on the power of interleaving, the implication is an obvious one: all major exams in your course should be cumulative. Research on learning supports this implication. In one recent study of cumulative versus noncumulative exams in psychology courses, researchers analyzed the scores of students in a cluster of psychology courses on a postcourse assessment; students who had taken a cumulative final exam scored substantially higher on the postcourse assessment than those who had taken noncumulative finals (Khanna, Brack, and Finken 2013). In some of the courses, the positive learning effects of the cumulative final exam persisted as long as 18 months after the completion of the course.

More generally, every major assignment should require students to draw—at least a little bit—on information or concepts or skills they have learned in previous units. This does not have to mean that the third exam of the course must be divided into three parts, one on each of the first three units. It may be that the third exam focuses primarily on the third unit, with two-thirds or three-quarters of the tested material deriving from that section of the course. But the final third or quarter should require students to return to material from earlier parts of the course. You can even accomplish this in a less obvious way by giving assignments or asking exam questions that require students to compare current content or skills with previously learned material. In my literature survey course, which divides into four units over the course of the semester, each exam requires students to answer three or four large essay questions. After the first exam, one of those questions always requires them to compare an author or event or trend from the current period with one from a previous period. They are warned about this, which gives me an opportunity to remind them about the importance of continually returning to the authors and ideas we have already discussed.

Quizzes represent another excellent opportunity to leverage the power of interleaving in your courses. Select some reasonable percentage of your quizzes that will be devoted to previously covered material, and stick with it throughout the semester. If you give 10-question multiple-choice quizzes on a weekly basis, set aside two questions for previously learned material. If you give one-question writing-based quizzes, as I do, ensure that every third or fourth quiz requires students to return to previously learned material. This is especially important to do if you make your exams cumulative, as of course you should. The more students are asked to return to previous material on the quizzes, the better they will be prepared to do so on the exams. Overall, you should consider your total package of quizzes and exams as the ideal tool for continuously reinforcing learned material from the first week of the semester to the last. If you don't give a cumulative final exam, you are essentially conveying to students that what they learned in the first weeks of the semester doesn't matter anymore. If you do give a cumulative final exam but not cumulative mid-terms or quizzes that test them on previously learned material, you are not giving them the kind of help they really need to solidify and enhance their early-semester learning on the cumulative exams.

I would be omitting a truth you would quickly discover on your own if I did not reiterate at this point that students might not respond with unbridled enthusiasm (at least initially) to these kinds of modifications to your assessment plan. Just as I felt frustration when I first began to test myself on previously learned Spanish vocabulary and quickly realized how little of it I remembered, your students might feel initial frustration at the expectation that everything they have learned remains on the table for all of their quizzes and exams. Maryellen Weimer, in a post on cumulative exams on the website Faculty Focus (Weimer 2015), offered some excellent suggestions for helping reconcile students to cumulative exams, all of which sit perfectly within the framework of small teaching activities, requiring just a small investment of class time:

· Open each class session by posting a test question from a previous exam or a potential test question related to previous course content. Give students time to consider and discuss their answers.

- Close class sessions by asking students to create a test question based on that day's material, and pose that question back to them in future class sessions.
- Open or close class sessions by asking students to open their notebooks to a previous day's class session and underline the three most important principles from that day; allow a few moments for a brief discussion of what they featured from their notes.

Strategies like these give you the opportunity to announce to students from the beginning of the semester that all learning in the course will be cumulative, and they give your students the help they need in preparing to succeed on cumulative exams.

Mixing Classroom Learning

You might remember that one of the suggestions made in the first chapter was to use opening questions that required students to remind you what you did in the previous class, week, or unit of the course. That recommendation was made in the service of giving your students practice in retrieving previously taught information. However, now you will recognize that it also contributes to an interleaved approach to the material, since Wednesday's class will induce them to return to Monday's material, and so on. Asking questions about previous material (e.g., in the form of the test questions recommended by Weimer 2015) would constitute a very low-level form of interleaving and can be easily supplemented or enhanced by more substantive exercises. For example, teachers of science, technology, engineering, and mathematics (STEM) classes, which include problem solving as one of the major learning activities, often ask students to complete homework problems prior to class and then open the next class with a brief review of those problems or the opportunity for students to ask questions about them and clarify answers. In most cases, following this brief review, the class will then move on to the new topic and leave those problems behind. A very slight modification to this traditional strategy—the essence of small teaching—would help provide that interleaving boost. Assume for a moment that the students worked on problems the previous evening and now are sitting in your class ready to review them and ask a few questions. You spend those first few minutes on questions and review as usual. Then, before moving on to the new material for that day's class, you give them one more new problem to complete right there in class. Make it a quick one so it doesn't eat up too much class time, but doing this will give them one more (distributed) opportunity to practice the problem-solving skill that you introduced in the last class period.

Thinking more generally about how you divide up your course material, you might consider a change that requires no new techniques or strategies—just a small (teaching) shift in how you introduce the material in chronological terms. A common organizational structure in any problem-based course would be to spend the bulk of the class working on a single idea or problem type and then to give students a little time at the end to work independently on a problem of that type. This is a sensible enough structure, and if you are indeed giving them time at the end of class to work on problems you are doing something good already (as we shall see in Chapter 5). An alternative to this structure would be to divide the class session into two halves, each of which focuses on a different topic, with the problem-solving session coming in the middle. So Monday's class might begin with a review of the material covered on Friday and addressed in the homework, followed by a 10-minute problem-solving session—which will have the added benefit of breaking the class at the midway point and renewing student attention for the second half of class. In that second half, you introduce new material. They do homework on that material for Wednesday, which begins with a review and then problem-solving session, and so on. The contrast between these two approaches would look like this:

Blocked Class Sessions	Interleaved Class Sessions
Monday: Topic A, Problem-Solving Session	Topic A, Problem-Solving Session, Topic B
Wednesday: Topic B, Problem-Solving Session	Topic B, Problem-Solving Session, Topic C
Friday: Topic C, Problem-Solving Session, Quiz	Topic C, Problem-Solving Session, Review or Quiz

The potential objection you might have to this approach would be that Topic A takes a full 40 or 60 minutes to explain and introduce. Remember, though, that asking students to struggle a little bit with material that they have not fully mastered will help draw on the learning power of prediction. In addition, interleaving can produce initial feelings of frustration in learners, precisely because they don't have the opportunity for full mastery before moving to the next thing. A little discomfort on either your part or the part of the students is not a bad thing as long as you can ultimately get beyond it and get into deeper learning.

Online Learning Environments

In *Minds Online*, Miller argued that online learning environments provide an ideal tool for creating interleaved learning experiences for our students. As we saw in the first chapter, she recommended the strategy of "staggered online deadlines that ensure spaced rather than massed work" (Miller 2014, p. 109). In a fully online course, she suggested that instructors "set up a recurring weekly schedule where each kind of work (discussion, quizzing, homework, any higher-stakes assignments such as major exams or papers) is due on a different day. You can set things up so that students are welcome to work ahead, but can't fall behind; some will manage to mass their work anyway by turning everything in extremely early, but those students are exceedingly rare" (p. 109). Exceedingly. For the majority of our students the use of such staggered deadlines will have the desired effect, especially if material from different weeks or units regularly appears in the various assessments. Miller noted that "when you prioritize spacing and interleaving in your course design, you create a much more complex set of deadlines for students" (p. 110), which may lead to hardships for students who sought out the online learning environment because they needed a more flexible learning schedule. Here, as in many areas of teaching, you may not be able to distribute deadlines quite as much as the literature on interleaving would recommend. Even a small bit of attention to the distribution of deadlines and spacing of material should help, though.

For blended courses, you might think about how the class and online components can work jointly to combine blocked and interleaved learning. Perhaps in your face-to-face sessions you concentrate on specific topics or skills, blocking those into your 50- or 75-minute sessions with your students. Especially if you meet the students only once per week in person, you might find you need to use that space for blocked learning to give them enough initial mastery and confidence to tackle the online work. In those online assignments and discussion boards, in addition to directing them to the recently covered material, you could continually push students back to older material or ask them to draw connections between the material covered in a recent class and previously covered material. You can also make use of staggered deadlines to help get the most power from those online components. You can just as easily reverse this strategy, giving online assignments in ways that will focus their attention on specific skills and using your face-to-face time to require them to mix practice and pull skills and ideas from throughout the course. Neither approach seems inherently better to me; it likely depends on the type of material you are teaching. However, it seems to me like a natural fit to make deliberate use of face-to-face and online course components to support both blocked and interleaved learning, whether you are doing so in a fully blended course or even in a traditional face-to-face course that uses any of the features of a learning management system, including quizzes or discussion boards. All these recommendations represent small design shifts that can be addressed as you are laying out the basic plan for your course.

PRINCIPLES

As you devise your own techniques to incorporate the power of interleaving into your courses, remember that you can use both spaced (or distributed) learning and interleaving to boost long-term retention. The smallest teaching step would be to find simple ways to space out student exposure to key course material through cumulative quizzes and exams. If you see positive results, you can then work more gradually on how to design an assessment system that creates more fully interleaved learning.

Block AND Interleave Blocked learning sessions probably form the backbone of the course plan for many instructors, including me. The research cited in this chapter does not require you to subtract blocked learning sessions from your course; it recommends that you add interleaving to them. To gain some initial mastery of new content or a novel skill, learners may well need some initial sessions of blocked or massed practice, as the experiment with students learning French pronunciation would suggest (Carpenter and Mueller 2013). Don't hesitate to dig into a focused problem-solving session or to spend concentrated periods of time introducing new content. Just ensure that students return to that material over and over again throughout the semester, encountering it in multiple contexts so that they can continually develop and refine their knowledge and skills.

Keep It Small, Keep It Frequent As with retrieval practice, frequency matters when it comes to interleaving. Students should have the opportunity to return to key course concepts or skills multiple times over the course of the semester, both in class and on their assessments. If you provide at least one opportunity for interleaving in every class period, and on every quiz or exam, you should be able to cycle back to major elements of the course several times. To help you accomplish this task, keep your interleaving sessions in class small. As with prediction and retrieval, you can use the opening and closing minutes of class to link students to previous course content or even to point them toward future content. Use those windows to pose and discuss previous test or assignment questions, have them solve an additional problem, or highlight and review older material.

Explain and Support Learning through interleaving can seem frustrating to learners, at least initially. In experiments in which learners have the opportunity to learn through blocked or interleaved practice, they overwhelmingly choose blocked practice because it gives them a feeling of mastery over the material. Pausing before you have fully mastered something can feel frustrating, as can be the demand to recall material or practice skills you thought you had mastered but then realize you don't know as well as you had imagined. Make sure that you speak to your students about the benefits of interleaving, about the nature of your assessments, and about the differences between short- and long-term learning. You might find that initially student grades on cumulative exams are lower, and consider giving less weight in the overall course grade to early exams, allowing the students an exam or two to accustom themselves to the challenging nature of interleaved learning.

SMALL TEACHING QUICK TIPS: INTERLEAVING

We can once again look to those fertile opening and closing minutes of the class period for interleaving techniques. But every one of your assessments, from quizzes to papers and tests and presentations, can become a potent tool in your interleaving arsenal.

- Reserve a small part of your major exams (and even the minor ones, such as quizzes) for questions or problems that require students to draw on older course content.
- Open or close each class session with small opportunities for students to retrieve older knowledge, to practice skills developed earlier in the course, or to apply old knowledge or skills to new contexts.
- Create weekly mini review sessions in which students spend the final 15 minutes of the last class session of the week applying that week's content to some new question or problem.
- Use quiz and exam questions that require students to connect new material to older material or to revise their understanding of previous content in light of newly learned material.
- In blended or online courses, stagger deadlines and quiz dates to ensure that students benefit from the power of spaced learning.

CONCLUSION

Interleaving brings us to the conclusion of the Knowledge section of the book, but the benefits of interleaving are not restricted to the memorization of fact or the mastery of content. As some of the experiments described here demonstrate, interleaving improves long-term retention in all areas of learning, from retention of facts to the mastery of higher order cognitive skills. It will prove as effective in your students' memorization of key concepts in your discipline as it will in their mastery of complex skills like writing, speaking, or problem solving. This chapter serves as an excellent transition from knowledge to understanding since an interleaved approach to learning should overlay all of your course design and teaching practices.

In short, if you want students to do well on your individual quizzes and exams and papers and projects, you can teach them through massed or blocked practice.

If you want them to learn content or skills that stretch across the entire semester, and even beyond the confines of your course, interleave.

Understanding

I devoted the introduction to Part I to convincing you that spending class time helping students acquire knowledge was time well spent—that we can't offload this crucial task to Google or expect previous courses to have taken care of that fundamental work. I probably don't need to kick off Part II by convincing you of the value of helping students to develop understanding, to improve their problem-solving skills, and to become more effective writers or presenters. You probably conceive of your role as a teacher primarily in terms of doing that work, as indeed you should. If you are reading this book—or any book like this one—you are also likely already a practitioner of teaching strategies that foster what we might label active learning, in which students spend at least some time *doing* things in the classroom rather than merely sitting there passively. However, the literature that you will see cited in the next three chapters suggests that to assist students in developing their comprehension or acquiring complex cognitive skills such as solving math problems or interpreting a poem, we have to do more than invite questions, hold discussions, use group work, or assign online drill work. We may certainly want to do some or all of these things—but if we do them, we must do them deliberately, with eyes wide open, and with the help of the literature on human learning. Too often, instructors assume that teaching by discussion (or group work or…) rather than lecturing will automatically translate into active learning, and deeper understanding. Unfortunately, this is not always the case.

The current term that springs to mind at the moment when college and university teachers think about active learning is the *flipped classroom*, which has become a catch-all phrase used to describe classroom structures in which students gain first exposure to course content outside of the classroom and then spend their time within the classroom doing things like solving problems, thinking critically, and writing. This structure—which has been standard operating procedure in many humanities classrooms for decades now—flips the traditional model of higher education in science, technology, engineering, and mathematics (STEM) disciplines, in which instructors provided first exposure through lectures in the classroom and then sent students off to *do* things outside of class. The explosion of new teaching technologies in recent years has enabled more and more instructors to flip their classrooms in this manner and has led to the rapid spread of flipped classrooms in American higher education—not to mention the rapid spread of positive publicity. A press release from a company that promotes learning resources designed for flipped classrooms reported triumphantly in 2013 that around half of all college and university teachers either have tried the flipped classroom or are planning to do so in the near future. Further, "among those employing it already, 57 percent of faculty agrees that their flipped classroom is 'extremely successful' or 'successful'" (Sonic Foundry 2013). This could strike us as a positive development, given that the majority of instructors are having a positive experience with bringing active learning strategies into their classrooms. But even without being a math professor, I can note that this survey result means that 43 percent of instructors using a flipped classroom approach are seeing either no improvement in learning or even reduced learning from their gymnastic (and often work-intensive and time-consuming) restructuring of their classrooms.

Robert Talbert, a mathematician and regular contributor to the *Chronicle of Higher Education* who writes frequently about flipped classrooms, noted correctly that opening up the classroom to cognitive activities (rather than simply lecturing and presenting information) represents nothing more than a framing strategy that can have very mixed results:

> The flipped classroom does not automatically provide ... outstanding learning experiences. What it provides is *space* and *time* for instructors to design learning activities and then carry them out, by relocating the transfer of information to outside the classroom. But then the instructor has the responsibility of using that space and time effectively. And sometimes that doesn't work. [Italics in original] (Talbert 2014)

Careful and strategic design, in other words, matters in the flipped classroom as much as it matters in every other type of classroom, from a large class lecture to a small seminar discussion. I have been teaching the literature professor's version of the flipped classroom since the start of my career now; students read literary texts before class and then come to class and we talk about how to interpret them. But I have walked away from far too many of these discussions, even lively and interesting ones, wondering whether anyone *learned* anything—and especially, whether anyone had acquired something looking like a skill that would help them write their papers or take their exams more effectively. This applies in the flipped classroom: just because students are busily working away at tasks at their desks doesn't mean they are learning anything.

I still remember a Renaissance literature course I took as an undergraduate in which the instructor put us in small groups with instructions to discuss key passages of whatever text we were studying that day. I loathed those sessions, saw them as pointless, and can assure you I learned nothing from them. Looking back now, through the lens of many years of teaching and reading about teaching and learning in higher education, I can see multiple problems with the way those sessions worked: we had no real task to complete, beyond the vague injunction to discuss the passages; the teacher offered no guidance or supervision while we worked and instead did something inscrutable up at the front of the room; and although a connection may have existed, she did not articulate for us any connection between what we were doing in those group sessions and what we did on our essays or exams. Talbert pointed out that good flipped classroom learning requires frequent interaction between the instructor and the students; he described it as "the kind of interactive engagement that a coach might have with his or her players while they practice. The coach doesn't do the exercises *for* the players, but neither does s/he stand off to the side and let them flail around the entire time" (Talbert 2014). Just so. But we all have likely encountered ineffective coaches, so the matter is even more complex than this. Certain kinds of interactions and feedback are more likely to promote learning than others, just as certain kinds of cognitive activities are more likely to promote learning than others.

The three chapters in this section offer small teaching strategies designed to help you foster active learning moments in your classroom—whether you think about those moments as flipping or not—in ways that are brief, powerful, and supported by the research on human learning. Any one of the strategies you'll find in these three chapters could become the basis for a full- or even multiclass activity, and the strategies often do serve that function in my own classroom. However, I have tried in the Models section of each chapter to provide examples and ideas for how they could fit into the framework of small teaching. Some of them describe how to conclude a class session with a 10- or 15-minute small teaching activity, and you might think about those activities as the most appropriate ways to conclude a lecture or discussion. But the three major concepts in this part of the book—connecting, practicing, and self-explaining—could also serve as key design principles for a flipped class session, for effective group work interactions, or for creating homework assignments or other online activities. An instructor can create opportunities for self-explanation, for example, as easily in an online homework environment as she can do so in group work tasks or in brief skill-based practice activities. The principle matters more than the specific form in which it manifests itself.

The small teaching approaches described in Part I all centered on helping students gain a strong knowledge foundation through effective first exposure and then carefully planned sequencing and repetition. Building learning, though, doesn't quite work like building a house, as we saw in our chapter on interleaving. You don't need or even want to completely master one cognitive activity before moving to the next one. Similarly, as students are developing their knowledge base, they should also be exploring and testing methods to use that knowledge for a wider range of cognitive activities. The following chapters will give you a set of small teaching tools for creating classroom or online experiences that deepen student understanding, improve the ability of your students to analyze and improve their own learning, and become mindful practitioners of a range of cognitive skills.

Chapter 4

Connecting

INTRODUCTION

Although you probably know him solely as the author of *Animal Farm* and *1984*, British writer George Orwell produced a massive amount of fiction and nonfiction in his lifetime; his complete body of published and unpublished writing totals more than 8,000 pages. Since my disciplinary research in British literature focuses partly on Orwell's work, I've read much (though not quite all) of Orwell's writings, including *A Clergyman's Daughter*, a novel that was little read when it was published and perhaps even less read now. I count it as one of my favorite of Orwell's works, though he had a different opinion of it; he disliked it so much that he forbade it to be republished, after the original printing, during his lifetime. The novel's protagonist is Dorothy Hare, the daughter of a selfish and indifferent rector living in the English countryside in the early part of the twentieth century. Dorothy undergoes a traumatic incident in the first half of the novel that results in her waking up in London with total amnesia. After bouts of homelessness and seasonal farm work, she finally winds up as a teacher in a small private school outside of the city. When she first encounters her new pupils, who range in age from 5 or 6 to their late teens, she concludes with despair that the mechanical and rote methods of instruction of their previous teachers have been spectacularly ineffective. Whatever knowledge the students have consists of "small disconnected islets" (Orwell 1986, p. 209) in a vast sea of ignorance. Those scattered bits don't add up to much: "It was obvious that whatever they knew they had learned in an entirely mechanical manner, and they could only gape in a sort of dull bewilderment when asked to think for themselves" (p. 209).

I don't find my students gaping at me too often in dull bewilderment. But Orwell's description of Dorothy's students—one that likely stemmed from the several years he spent teaching at an English boarding school—caught my attention when I first read it because it does capture an experience I have encountered in the classroom more times than I would care to count. It typically happens when I begin pressing students to make connections between disparate sets of concepts or skills in a course—asking them, in other words, to build bridges between the disconnected islets described by Orwell. For example, when we are tackling a new author in my British literature survey course, I might begin class by pointing out some salient feature of the author's life or work and asking students to tell me the name of a previous author (whose work we have read) who shares that same feature. "This is a Scottish author," I will say. "And who was the last Scottish author we read?" Blank stares. Perhaps just a bit of gaping bewilderment. Instead of seeing the broad sweep of British literary history, with its many plots, subplots, and characters, my students see Author A and then Author B and then Author C and so on. They can analyze and remember the main works and features of each author, but they run into trouble when asked to forge connections among writers.

That problem is especially acute at the beginning of a semester. In *How Learning Works*, Susan Ambrose and her co-authors offer a clear explanation for that by noting the different ways novices and experts in a field process and position new knowledge. Experts, they explained, have a much richer "density of connections among the concepts, facts, and skills they know" (Ambrose, Bridges, DiPietro, Lovett, and Norman 2010, p. 49). When they encounter a new piece of information or a new idea in their field of expertise, they immediately slot it into a fully developed network that enables them to see connections between it and dozens of other things they know. When I encounter a new work in recent British literature, then, I can immediately see how it connects to other similar works, to major events in British history, to a specific region of Britain, or even to current events there. My students, by contrast, are novice learners in the field; their knowledge of it, to borrow a phrase from *How Learning Works*, is "sparse and superficial" (p. 46). Especially at the beginning of a semester, Ambrose et al. explained, students might" absorb the knowledge from each lecture in a course without connecting the information to other lectures or recognizing themes that cut across the course" (p. 49). They don't know enough about British history to understand that Scotland and England have a complex and fraught history and that therefore we might find connecting threads between Scottish authors in terms of how they portray their neighbors to the south.

In short, they have knowledge, in the sense that they can produce individual pieces of information in specific contexts; what they lack is understanding or comprehension.

And they lack comprehension, even more shortly, because they lack connections.

IN THEORY

James Zull is a biologist whose career took an interesting new turn when he began to reflect on how a better understanding of the biology of the brain could help teachers do their work more effectively.

The title of his first book, *The Art of Changing the Brain: Enriching the Practice of Teaching by Exploring the Biology of Learning* (Zull 2002), articulates nicely the major point he wants teachers to understand: when we learn anything new, we are making changes to our brains. When we are helping other people learn new things, like our students, we are making changes to their brains. It would seem only natural, then, that a little bit of understanding of how brains work should accompany our efforts to change them. Since the last science course I took was Concepts in General Science more than 25 years ago, you can imagine how welcome I find books like Zull's, which translate the research of brain researchers into imagery and language accessible to English professors like me.

To understand the link between *making connections* and *building comprehension*, on which this chapter focuses, consider for a moment Zull's depiction of what happens when we learn. Our brains are filled with cells called neurons, which do the work of what we call thinking. A human brain has at least 100 billion neurons, and those neurons contain branching structures called axons that allow them to communicate with other neurons; they do so not by touching the tips of the axons together (as in a handshake) but through the release of chemical neurotransmitters into a tiny space between one neuron and the next called a synaptic gap. As Zull puts it, in his folksy way, neurons "make friends easily" (Zull 2002, p. 96). A single neuron can form literally tens of thousands of connections with other neurons, both near and far away. (The axons, he explains, can extend as far as 6 feet.) Neurons form new connections with one another with every new experience we have: new sensations, new thoughts, new actions. As the neurons are connecting to one another in novel ways, growing and strengthening new connections, they are forming networks. The first time neurons link up in a new way, that connection is a temporary or fleeting one; if that connection is used again (because we repeat the thought, or recreate an experience), the link strengthens. The more times the pathway is used, the stronger the connection. Neurons that fire together, goes the saying in this corner of the biological world, wire together (Lang 2013, p. 114).

With that brief summary of your brain under our belts, we can now better understand Zull's explanation of how learning constitutes a change in our brain—a change, more particularly, to our neuronal networks: "The knowledge in our minds consists of neuronal networks in our brains, so if that knowledge is to grow, the neuronal networks must physically change. This is the change that a teacher wants to create. It is change in connections … unless there is some change in connections, no learning can occur" (Zull 2002, p. 112). According to this definition, we learn when our brains form new neuronal networks or modify existing ones as a result of our experiences; this means that, quite literally, learning requires the continual formation of new connections between our neurons. Think back to the image that Orwell gave us, which now seems quite apt: an individual and isolated piece of knowledge, one that students can't do much with, is exactly like a disconnected islet—just as Dorothy observed in her students. It has few connections to other neuronal networks in our brain. An initial neuronal connection might form when a teacher tells us some piece of information and will fire again in a very small and limited range of circumstances. A piece of knowledge that we understand thoroughly, however, and that we can reflect deeply on and apply to new contexts and more, will have connections to lots of other neuronal networks. It might have come in from the teacher, but then we recognized how it related to something we already knew; we thought about it when we saw something similar in a movie later that day; later still we were able to use it in an essay we were writing. Each of those new uses of that piece of information connected it to another set of networks, until it eventually sits at the heart of a dense weave of connections—what we normally think about as understanding or comprehension.

Hence, a simple way of understanding how to build comprehension in our students would be that it consists of helping them forge rich, interconnected networks of knowledge—ones that enable each existing piece of information in our content area to connect with lots of other information, concepts, and ideas. Shifting our language from the biology of the brain to the ways we normally think about student comprehension, we want them to have rich frameworks of knowledge in our content areas, ones that enable them to connect and organize information in meaningful and productive ways. In the past several chapters we have considered how we can help students form and strengthen primary new connections in their brains—creating strong wiring that will allow them to retrieve course content when they need it. In this chapter we consider how we expand those connections into networks that enable students to see the bigger picture, make meaning, apply what they have learned into novel contexts, and more. Our role as teachers now expands as well: we want to facilitate the process of students making connections. Ambrose et al. argued that the primary difference between teachers and students lies in the realm of connections: "One important way experts' and novices' knowledge organizations differ is in the number or density of connections among the concepts, facts, and skills they know" (Ambrose, Bridges, DiPietro, Lovett, and Norman 2010, p. 49). As an expert in your discipline, your network is thick with connections. As a teacher in your discipline, your task is to help your students develop a denser, more richly connected network of knowledge and skills in your course content areas.

As a further illustration of this notion, consider a famous little study on memory that was conducted by British psychologists in the early 1980s (Morris, Gruneberg, Sykes, and Merrick 1981). The researchers in this case showed a list of football (soccer) scores to more than a hundred undergraduates at the beginning of a lecture; they were not told to memorize them, however. After a brief interval the students were given a test designed to check their knowledge of football, with questions like this: "Who is manager of Birmingham city?" The lecturer than showed them the list of teams from the beginning of the session and asked them to fill in the scores they had been shown previously. When the researchers compared the results of the two tests, they found that a stronger understanding of football corresponded with a better ability to remember the scores. This experiment is usually used to illustrate the importance of prior knowledge on our learning of new material, something we will get to in just a moment.

But if you reflect on what happened in this experiment, you can see how it provides a handy demonstration of the power of connections. The students who had a general knowledge of football would have been able to assign meaning to the scores they had been shown, and that meaning would have come in the form of connections between the scores and other things they knew about those scores. For example, they might have noticed that one score represented an upset: a team with a historically poor record had upended a championship-caliber team. Or they might have remembered that one of the teams had recently acquired a star player and thought about how that star player could have affected the outcome of the game or about how a particular score meant that a team was going to advance to the playoffs, which were coming up. In all of these cases, what the knowledgeable students had was a rich network of connections among lots of different facts about football—individual players and their histories, the current and past win–loss records of favorite teams, recent trades—and that rich network of connections enabled them to take in the *new* piece of information (i.e., the football score) and put it into a meaningful place. The more we can help students develop rich networks in our content areas, the more we enable them to build meaning and comprehension of what we are teaching them.

We have to note an essential qualification here. You can't fire the synapses in your students' brains. For the connections to be meaningful and effective, the students have to form them. Your task is to create an environment that facilitates the formation of those connections rather than simply lecturing at them about connections. Believe me, I speak to my British literature students about connections between various authors and events in British literary history all the time. However, just telling them about those connections isn't enough. They have to build up the connected networks in their own brains—with our help. An excellent illustration of this notion comes from another intriguing experiment conducted on psychology students. In this case students were given, in advance of class, either a complete set of notes on the lecture for the day or a partial set of notes—one that consisted of "headings and titles of definitions and concepts, which required students to add information to complete the notes" (Cornelius & Owen-DeSchryver 2008, p. 8). So the students who received the full notes had the knowledge network for the day handed to them prior to class (through the course learning management system); the students who received the partial notes received only the frame of that knowledge network, and had to fill in the rest on their own. The students in both conditions performed comparably on the first two examinations for the course. On the third and final examinations, however, as the amount of course material increased and required deeper understanding, the students in the partial-notes condition outperformed their full-note peers. Especially relevant for the argument that connections improve comprehension, the students in the partial-notes condition outperformed their peers on conceptual questions on the final exam. As the authors explained, "On a [final] test that required knowledge of a large number of concepts, rote memorization was not feasible, so students who encoded the information by actively taking notes throughout the semester may have performed better because they had experienced better conceptual understanding" (p. 10). This experiment has obvious implications for classroom teaching, or even the creation of reading guides or lecture notes for an online courses. However, the important point for now is that the partial notes gave students an *organized framework* that enabled and encouraged them to *see and make new connections* on their own.

One final takeaway from this explanation of connections and their role in learning is that the prior knowledge that students bring into a course or class period has an obvious influence on their learning. Although you might think your students know absolutely nothing about your subject on the first day of class, that's probably not true. They know—or think they know—something: they might have folk theories or a simplistic understanding of key terms. When you first begin presenting information and ideas to them, then, their synapse-forming brains will start to search for connections between what they already know and what they are hearing. Much has been made of the ways poor or inaccurate prior knowledge can interfere with their new learning; as Zull explains, you can't make existing connections in people's brains disappear (Zull 2002, pp. 105–106). Instead of attempting this futile task, or ignoring their prior knowledge completely, the universally recommended strategy to address this issue is to surface and address their prior knowledge. Asking students to activate what they already know about a subject before they learn it more deeply helps light up the connections that they already have (just as prediction activities can do) and will give you a better understanding of where you might need to start in terms of your presentation of new material. If that prior-knowledge-surfacing process reveals deep misconceptions, you might have to work more deliberately to demonstrate to students the inadequacy of their connections and help them form more accurate and productive ones. Without undertaking some effort to discover and assess whatever prior knowledge they might have about your subject, you might find that their existing networks distort new information to make it fit with what they already know rather than using it to build up rich and productive new networks.

MODELS

Strategies to help students modify and enhance their connections can fall at any point during the semester or during any class period. The following four strategies include opportunities for students to activate prior knowledge at the beginning of the semester, to build connected networks throughout the semester with and without technology, and to prepare for final exams and projects as they are finishing the semester. Small teaching here takes the form not only of brief activities within and outside of the classroom but also of single-class activities that will help students forge connections within a semester's worth of material.

What Do You Already Know (and What Do You Want to Know?)

As noted already, the existing intellectual connections of your students represent a valuable and important starting point for helping them build new knowledge networks in your subject area. "Prior knowledge plays a critical role in learning," explain Susan Ambrose and Marsha Lovett, "which means that ... faculty members need to assess the content, beliefs and skills students bring with them into courses and ... use that information as both a foundation for new learning as well as an opportunity to intervene when content knowledge is inaccurate or insufficient"

(Ambrose & Lovett 2014, p. 16). Essentially, you want to ask your students to make individual and collective knowledge dumps, telling you everything they know—or think they know—about your subject before you begin teaching them. This not only will help you recognize and correct mistaken perceptions they have but will also activate whatever knowledge they currently have that you want to build on or reinforce. In that sense, it has a function similar to the kinds of prediction activities discussed in Chapter 2, in that it fertilizes the intellectual soil for the knowledge and skills that you will help them to develop in the coming days and weeks. The strategy for soliciting and addressing existing knowledge networks need not be a complicated one: simply ask them about it. You could do this in multiple ways that fit the frame of small teaching:

- Prior to class, ask students to take a prequiz or respond to two or three questions about the subject matter on the course's learning management system and then summarize those results briefly at the start of the first or second class.
- At the start of any individual class period, ask students to spend 5 minutes writing down what they think they already know about the subject; take another 5 minutes to solicit some responses and discuss them.
- At the start of the semester, devote part of one class period to assessing students' current state of knowledge, either through whole-class or group activities or through a written pretest (a strategy that also fits well with what we learned about the learning power of prediction).
- At the close of the first class of the semester, after you have introduced the subject matter and the course, ask students to write down three questions they have about the subject matter or three things they would like to learn over the course of the semester. Discuss their responses in the second class.

Once you have heard what students have to offer in such an exercise and have thus gained a glimpse into their existing networks, you can strategize how to build upon them most effectively in the course.

As an example of the third suggestion, when I teach a seminar on twenty-first-century British literature and culture, I set aside 30 minutes on the first day of the semester for a knowledge dump in which students respond to the following question: "When I say the word 'British,' what are the primary impressions that form in your mind?" I pose this question and give them a few minutes to make a list on paper, and then we fill up the board with their impressions. I try to categorize their impressions so we can see patterns—and the same basic patterns always emerge. *British* to them means the royal family, traditional activities like having tea and biscuits or taking long walks in the country, green landscapes and ruined castles. The more culturally sophisticated among them will throw in contributions like the Beatles or Ricky Gervais. None of them ever mention the ethnic diversity of Britain or the fact that *Britishness* encompasses the peoples of Scotland and Wales and Northern Ireland or its recent political history. The second class period, in which we begin considering the political and cultural context of British literature, then gives me an opportunity not to dismiss their impressions but to demonstrate how limiting they are and to begin to connect them to the parts of Britishness that they have never encountered. Throughout the semester I will occasionally return to the impressions we laid out on that first day and remind them about how our current text or discussion connects back to them. Such an opening-class activity can obviously work in almost any type of course, modified in ways that best fit your inclinations. For an upper-level course you might want to narrow down the questions, since they might have more general extensive knowledge than would fit into a paragraph. The overall strategy here remains happily simple: prior to the introduction of any major new chunk of course content, spend a class period (for a whole course) or a few minutes (for a new unit) asking them what they already know.

Provide the Framework

As you are providing first exposure to students, in the form of either your lecture or their readings, help them avoid Orwell's disconnected islets (Orwell 1986, p. 209) by providing them with the organizing framework of the material and letting them fill in the details. As we saw in one of the aforementioned studies, giving students an organizing framework with hierarchies and key concepts in advance of the lecture helped students master conceptual questions on the final exam more effectively than giving them a full set of completed notes. This strategy enables you to help them build accurate connections without simply handing them an already completed network and without leaving them to devise the organizational principles of the material on their own (which, as novice learners, they will have trouble doing). As the researchers in the experiment did, you can make such an outline available online for students to print out and bring to class; you could hand it out at the beginning of class; you could require students in an online environment to complete such an outline as they watch videos or complete required online readings. Another option in a traditional environment would be to write the skeletal outline and key terms on the board prior to the start of class, which would take just a few minutes. Make sure that students understand not to simply copy down the entire outline from the start but to use it as a guide as they take their notes throughout the class. My observations of instructors in multiple disciplines throughout the past dozen years or more has suggested to me that most of us don't think very strategically about the positive role that boards can play in student learning. We tend either to cover them with our notes or to use them to write down ideas or comments that strike us as important in that moment. Setting aside a small section of the board that contains an organizing framework and facilitates students taking meaningful notes and building up rich knowledge networks could help provide some meaning to that kind of impressionistic board use.

Overall, when it comes to providing students with the material from your slides of your lecture or any other course content, remember that smaller is better; you will help them connect most deeply if you provide only the outline and let them do the rest of the work.

Concept Maps

A rich literature exists on the use of concept maps (also sometimes called mind maps), which present a fast and easy method to help students visualize the organization of key ideas in your course. I like the use of concept maps in particular for group exercises, since group work so often falters when students have not been given a clear task with a concrete outcome, or been given a task that they find too easy or too challenging. The creation of a concept map is a manageable task for a small group of students to undertake at the conclusion of a lesson or a unit of material and offers the additional benefit of being an interesting and (in the best of all possible worlds) even enjoyable activity. The phrase *concept map* essentially describes the activity; Ambrose et al. defined a concept map simply as "a visual representation of a knowledge domain" (Ambrose, Bridges, DiPietro, Lovett, and Norman 2010, p. 63). Concept maps can be constructed on sheets of paper, on posters, on tablets or computers with or without the help of concept-mapping software. One can use concept maps to allow students to construct a visual depiction of everything they know, with key concepts located in boxes or circles in the center of the map and then lines branching off of those central concepts or ideas to other subsidiary elements: other concepts, supporting points or details, examples, and so on (think about the image of all those neurons connecting to each other in your brain). The lines between the different elements of a concept map can be labeled in ways that define the relationships between them.

An even better use of concept maps, though, is to provide students with a focus question to which the concept map comes as a response. So a historian might ask students to construct a concept map that demonstrates the positive and negative consequences of violent revolutions; an environmental scientist could assign a concept map that asks students to depict all of the consequences of some major climatological event. I have had my students create concept maps around the major characters in a single novel or around the appearance of a key theme in multiple novels. Even better still, follow the suggestion of *How Learning Works* and have students make multiple maps with different organizing principles. As the authors explain, "Giving students practice organizing their knowledge according to alternative schemata or hierarchies helps them see that different organizations serve different purposes and thus builds more robust and flexible knowledge organizations" (Ambrose, Bridges, DiPietro, Lovett, and Norman 2010, p. 63). If I ask students to create a map of novel characters one day, I might ask them to create one around its themes on a second day and yet another around its images on a third day.

Back in the age of the dinosaurs, I used to have my student groups construct concept maps by giving them blank overheads and asking them to create their maps with dry erase markers; this allowed us to spend the latter part of the class taking a quick look at everyone's maps on the overhead projector. Sometimes I still will ask students to do this, or I will stop at the bookstore before class and pick up some posters and markers and have them create their maps on a larger scale. But you might not prefer these ancient tools of the trade, or you might be teaching in an online environment, or you might have too many students to supervise and display all of the maps produced in your class. Fortunately, a wealth of free concept-mapping programs now exists for your students to create online versions of concept maps. Just search online for "free concept mapping," and you will find yourself with more options than you know what to do with. You can find programs to download and save to your device, and you can find websites that allow you to begin creating a new map instantly online. Some learning management systems even include concept-mapping options within them, so you might begin by checking there first if you are teaching in a blended or online environment. If your students already have devices in class, using technological tools for concept mapping will help you keep the activity small without worrying about using things like posters or overheads.

The Minute Thesis

After close to 20 years of teaching, and more than half that time studying and writing about teaching in higher education, I have had exactly one good idea for a teaching strategy that I can't trace back to anywhere else; everything else I have ever recommended, in this book or elsewhere, comes from someone or somewhere else. My single good idea consists of a game called the Minute Thesis, and it represents in some ways the germ of this book, in that it constitutes an ideal small teaching activity: free, easy, and capable of use in any size class, for any length of time you wish, from 10 minutes to the full class period. I began using it a dozen years ago as an attempt to help students at the end of the semester see connections across the various works we had read in an effort to develop ideas for their final papers—which mostly, in my classes, require them to do comparative analyses of several works from the course reading list. I wrote the name of the seven novels we had read on the board in a single column; in a second column, I wrote a list of themes that we had seen in various novels throughout the semester. I handed a marker to a student in the front row, asked her to walk up to the board and circle a single theme, and then asked her to draw lines connecting that theme to two different novels. Then I asked the students to spend 1 minute thinking about a thesis for an argument that would explain how those two novels connected to that theme. Some of them stared off into space, thinking; some of them actually wrote a phrase or sentence in their notebooks. After a minute (maybe 2), I asked them to tell me what they had come up with. A brief silence ensued (this always happens); then a tentative hand arose, and a tentative student made a tentative statement. I praised the student's idea and asked for another. More hands arose, more confidently, and more ideas emerged. After 5–10 minutes listening to the fascinating new set of connections that were emerging, I stopped the discussion and handed the marker to another student, asking him to circle a new theme and connect it to two different novels; the process then began anew. Over the course of a class period, the students created dozens of brief thesis statements that connected the novels and themes of the course in new and interesting ways, and many of the students took an idea they expressed in that class period and developed it into their final paper.

This brief little activity occurs in the final week of every class I teach now, as a way to help students solidify existing connections they have developed or envision new ones as they are preparing for their final papers or projects or the final exam. The potential variations in how you might conduct it are endless, as are the ways technology could modify or enhance it. You could, for example, use your course learning management system to start a handful of discussion threads that pair various course elements in different ways and ask each student to contribute a one-sentence thesis to that discussion thread over the course of a 24-hour period; to push their thinking even further, you might then assign students to articulate what the supporting evidence would look like under someone else's thesis. In the classroom you could likewise play out each iteration of the Minute Thesis further by selecting one thesis from those initially proffered and spending 10 minutes spelling out what the argument might look like. Or you could use three columns instead of two, requiring the students to think even more creatively about how to see the course material in newly connected ways. All that's really required is that you or the students set up columns or categories of essential course concepts or texts, connect them in new and creative ways, and then ask the students to describe how or why those connections make sense (or even don't make sense). In this way, just as in the practice of giving students an outline and key terms and letting them fill in their notes, you are offering the scaffolding through the columns or categories but then requiring students to make the connections themselves.

One final benefit of the minute thesis is that it can help students gain some practice in what might seem to them the mysterious process of coming up with new or original ideas—something we frequently ask of them when we assign papers or presentations or research projects. What we typically think about as "original" thinking usually means forging new connections between things that have not been connected before (Lang 2013, pp. 192–205). Ideas always have lineages, and those lineages can help us see the key role that creative connections play in the process of generating new thinking. Playing the minute thesis demystifies the process of coming up with new connections, and gives the students a tool they can use in all of their classes when they are trying to brainstorm ideas for their assignments.

PRINCIPLES

Connection exercises provide a bridge between your expert comprehension of your subject matter and the novice understanding of your students. As you consider how to help your students create their own connections, keep that primary focus in mind. You are helping your students obtain the big-picture view that informs and animates your grasp of the material.

Provide the Framework Remember that one of the most important ways your knowledge of the course content differs from your students lies in your ability to organize and connect concepts and information in meaningful ways. As you encounter new knowledge in your field, you can remember and work with it because of that organization. New learners in a field initially need lots of help in seeing the framework or organization of the material to be learned. You can help them by making the framework as visible as possible, pointing them back to it frequently, and helping them recognize where new material fits into the frame. The more familiar the students become with your course content, the less of this you will have to do.

Facilitate Connections The network of connections in your head doesn't transfer wholly into the heads of your students. Providing the frame to your students not only will help them better understand the organization of knowledge in your field but also leaves open the space for them to create the connections in their brains that will fuel deep learning. Be creative in developing techniques that allow students to see unexpected juxtapositions, chart new pathways through the material, or invent their own new knowledge networks. Be present as the guide and expert who can provide feedback on their discoveries, and help nudge them in productive new directions when they get stuck or stray too far from what you know works for experts in the field.

Leverage Peer Learning Power Of all the small teaching techniques considered in this book, this one lends itself most easily to the use of groups or peer learning activities. Your students all share the position of being novice learners in your field and can help each other understand how to build bridges between those disconnected islets. When you are providing opportunities for students to create connections, allow and encourage them to help each other. The process of creating connections lends itself to collaborative exercises that can revitalize the classroom and inject some fun into learning. The days on which we play the Minute Thesis game are always the most enjoyable ones of the semester; the room fills with energy and curiosity as the students make their own connections and consider the connections made by their peers.

SMALL TEACHING QUICK TIPS: CONNECTING

Making new connections is more complex than retrieving a remembered piece of information, so you may need to set aside more space and time in your course plans for connection exercises. Rather than trying to squeeze them into five- or ten-minute sessions in class, see if you can allot them more time in single-class sessions at the opening, midway point, or closing of the semester.

- Solicit the prior knowledge of your students at the beginning of the semester or individual class periods with brief written or oral questions or with whole-class knowledge dumps.
- Ask students to create concept maps that answer questions or solve problems; use concept maps multiple times throughout the semester with different organizational principles.
- Consider providing students only with the scaffolding or framework of lecture material in advance of class; let them fill in the framework with their own connections.

- As much as possible, offer examples or cases from everyday or common experience but also—and more importantly—give students the opportunity to provide such examples on their own.
- Consider using the Minute Thesis or other in-class activities that help students see or create new connections prior to major assignments or exams.

CONCLUSION

In *A Clergyman's Daughter*, protagonist Dorothy Hare discovers an ingenious method for connecting the disconnected islets of her students' minds in their history lessons. She buys a sheet of wallpaper, plasters it around the circumference of the room, and charges the students to fill it in with the events of English history. They leap into the task, filling in dates and characters and cutting out pictures and stories from illustrated papers to create a vast timeline of their national story. At long last, with the help of a simple framework provided by the teacher and the students' creation of their own connections, Dorothy's students begin truly learning.

Chapter 5

Practicing

INTRODUCTION

In spring 2007, I taught a course on contemporary British literature to a class of mostly junior and senior students. To supplement the novels and plays and poems we were reading with some broader cultural context, I asked each student to give a 10–15-minute presentation to the class on a British work of art in a popular genre. They could offer presentations on films, television shows, or even their favorite rock or rap recordings. I thought the assignment would elicit some strong work since it gave students the opportunity to present on topics in which they were interested—one student selected Pink Floyd's *The Wall*, another did the BBC television series *The Office*, and so on. Leading up to the days on which the presentations occurred, I gave the students a few tips on effective presentation techniques, enjoined them to practice at least two or three times before the final classes, and worked with some of them individually on the structure and organization of their material. I had high hopes, which were painfully dashed on presentation day. The students had clearly not practiced or timed their presentations out. The slides were poorly designed and crammed with text—which the students often read out word for word. The students were either nervous and stilted or overly casual and unpracticed. The presentations were supposed to last 10–12 minutes; one student spoke for more than 30, despite frequent injunctions to wrap things up. In fact, their work was so poor that I decided afterward I would never ask my students to give presentations again. I just couldn't stand the thought of sitting through another set of them.

However, in fall 2008 I agreed to teach a course in our honors program in which junior-year students produce a proposal for a thesis they would write during their senior year. The program requires that these juniors finish the course with an oral defense of their proposal—which meant that, just a semester after taking my no-presentation vow, I was stuck once again with observing and evaluating end-of-semester presentations. The stakes were now raised, though: each student in the class worked with a faculty mentor, who was asked to attend the defenses. This meant that presentations would take place in front of an audience of my peers. In part because of these raised stakes, and in part because of my previous experiences with presentations, I decided that I simply could not bear to sit through another set of unpracticed, ill-prepared, undertimed rambles. I had to do something to better prepare the students to succeed at these presentations. Unfortunately, I have no degree in public speaking and have never taught speech, so I didn't feel qualified to give detailed instructions on the finer points of designing presentations or public speaking. At the same time, I speak a lot in public. I do this not only as a professor speaking to students but also as a frequent guest speaker at faculty development workshops or lectures on other campuses. The one thing I have learned from that experience has been the value of repeated practice. The more times I give a specific lecture, or even mini lecture, the better it gets. Before I unveil any new material at a workshop, I have usually delivered it to my dog or to an empty classroom at least once or twice. As I have gained more experience as a speaker, I rely less on these practice sessions, but even now I still will usually run through the opening 5 minutes of a presentation at least two or three times.

This seemed to me like a gift I could give to my students as they prepared for their presentations. So as the final weeks of the semester in this honors class approached, I made an announcement to the students: "On the class before the presentations begin, you must be prepared to give the first 2 minutes of your presentation to the class. That's it—just the first 2 minutes. Rehearse it and be ready." With 15 students in a 75-minute class, and figuring time for transition and critique, that meant I had to give up one whole class period to this practice session—no content that day at all, just helping them improve their presentations. Given my previous experiences with the poor quality of student presentations, I was not at all sure that the effort would be worth the lost time. I still had no particular advice in mind to offer; my only real goal was to force the students to rehearse a few times, after which I hoped they would recognize the value of their rehearsals and do some additional practicing on their own.

Rehearsal day arrived. I selected a volunteer and asked the first student to begin. I let her speak for about three sentences, which were stiff and clearly memorized, before I stopped her.

"Hang on a second," I said. "Start over."

"Did I do something wrong?"

"Nope. I just want you to start over."

She began again, speaking a little more confidently. I let her go another few sentences.

"Wait," I said, interrupting again. She wore a pained expression. Students were looking at me, and at one another, with bewilderment.

"You're not doing anything wrong," I said. "But just start over again for me."

A chill descended on the room at that moment, as students began to wonder why I was torturing this poor women. Her third time around was much better, as she found her way into her own words, so I let her continue for a while. At the end of some technical explanation she gave about her material, I asked her to stop and describe it for me in her own words without looking at her notes. She put down her notes and broke out of the rigid posture in which she had been standing to explain what she meant. It came out a hundred times more clearly.

"That's better," I said. "Say it like that in the presentation."

"OK," she said, and then resumed her presentation where she had left off.

"No, no," I interrupted. "Say it like that *right now* in the presentation."

"Go back and do it again?" she said.

"Yes, go back and do it again. And don't look at your notes."

And so it went for the next 70 minutes, as I asked student after student to repeat false starts, clear up technical material or jargon, and put away written notes. The room went from a climate of fear and anxiety to one of laughter and relaxation as the students picked up on what was happening and saw that all I was trying to teach them were the virtues of practice and rehearsal. I can't say there were not a few bad moments. One student was so nervous and stammering it was painful to watch, and I thought interrupting her would do more harm than good. So I just let her talk. Eventually she realized that nobody was going to rescue her, and she locked in and worked her way through her nerves. The following week the students gave their presentations, and they were, by far, the best student talks I have ever seen. It could not have been clearer that every one of them had gone back to their rooms and rehearsed and timed themselves until they had it right. Some were better than others, but even the worst would have beaten out almost any presentation I had seen before.

IN THEORY

College classes frequently operate in a strange fashion if we think of them in contrast to other pursuits that human beings attempt to master. A professor spends a semester lecturing to her students about some complex subject matter. A good professor mixes those lectures with some active-learning strategies such as discussions and group exercises. But mostly in class the students are listening or talking. Then the first midterm period rolls around, and now the students are doing something quite different from listening or talking: they are writing essays, or answering multiple-choice questions, or designing presentations, or doing a variety of other complex cognitive activities that are distinct from the simple acts of talking or listening. If we taught students to play soccer in this way, it would entail putting them into the stands at a soccer game, lecturing to them about soccer, and encouraging them to have discussions about it. Then we might have them do a bunch of calisthenics. Then we would stick them in a stadium full of fans and tell them to play soccer. I suspect you would enjoy watching that soccer game about as much as I enjoyed watching my student presentations before I taught that honors class.

The small teaching strategy to be recommended in this chapter lies at the heart of this section and the heart of the book as a whole:

> Whatever cognitive skills you are seeking to instill in your students, and that you will be assessing for a grade, the students should have time to practice in class.

The trick in this recommendation lies in how specifically you identify the intellectual skills of that *whatever*. It may seem to you that holding an in-class discussion about a text serves as good preparation for writing an essay about that text. Those are two different things, though. To sit and listen to a discussion, contemplate ideas, and occasionally lob out one of your own constitutes something radically distinct from sitting down with an idea, parsing it out into pieces that can be separated into paragraphs, marshalling evidence for each paragraph, and so on. "It is virtually impossible to become proficient at a mental task," wrote cognitive psychologist Daniel Willingham, "without extended practice" (Willingham 2009, p. 107). If we want students to become proficient at the specific mental tasks that we are planning to assess—such as writing formal essays or responding to essay exam questions, writing lab reports, taking multiple-choice or true-false or short-answer exams—we have to give them extended practice at those tasks. Each of these types of assessments, and any other type of assessment you can dream up, requires students mastering a specific set of cognitive processes—none of them are exactly like any other. Students, like the rest of us, can demonstrate real mastery of one type of cognitive process while having little skill with a related one. You will perhaps know this from your experience meeting and working with students who can think very quickly on their feet in class discussions but can't write their way out of a paper bag, or those who can write brilliant essays but freeze and stammer when asked to respond to something quickly in class. This point was driven home to me firmly the year after I taught the honors class described above, when I became the director of the honors program and began teaching the writing-intensive introductory course for the program's first-year students. Sometimes I would read the terrible essays of a particular student and wonder how on earth he had been admitted to the program with such poor writing skills; then later on I would learn from one of my colleagues that she was brilliant at mathematics or science. My unspoken assumption had been that the really smart and talented kids would be able to master quickly any cognitive challenge we threw at them; my experience did not bear out this assumption.

Neither does the research of cognitive psychologists or learning theorists. "As far as anyone knows," wrote Willingham in *Why Don't Students Like School*, "the only way to develop mental facility [at a cognitive task] is to repeat the target process again and again" (Willingham 2009, p. 115). To explain why this is so, Willingham offered a very simple description of the process of thinking: "Thinking occurs when you combine information in new ways. That information might be drawn from the environment or from your long-term memory or from both" (p. 109). This process of combining mental inputs in new ways occurs in our working memories—which, unfortunately, have limited capacity. Willingham called them "a fundamental bottleneck of human cognition" (p. 109). And although we can improve our brain functioning and intelligence in some ways, we don't seem to be able to increase the size of our working memories very much; as far as we currently know, we have to work roughly with what we have been given. The fact that we run up against this fundamental limitation, however, does not mean that we cannot become better or more efficient at thinking. We can improve our "mental facility" at a cognitive task with practice—just as we improve our facility at any type of task, from hitting a softball to making an omelet. With cognitive tasks, practice helps us by lightening the load on our working memories. "Mental processes can become automatized," according to Willingham, and "automatic processes require little or no working memory" (p. 111). So if you have to complete some cognitive task that requires you to hold three or four elements in your working memory at the same time, practice might enable you to automatize one or two of those, thereby freeing up space for you to bring in other inputs from your long-term memory (e.g., instructions from your teacher) or your environment (e.g., the textbook in front of you). This will enable you to think more effectively or creatively as you combine ideas and information and processes in productive and interesting new ways.

Willingham gave the most frequently produced example of how this works in real learning tasks, pointing to research that has been done on math students who have memorized the times tables and those who have not. If you have the times tables memorized and do not have to pause and think about a simple multiplication equation while solving a problem, you can focus more effectively on the higher order thinking tasks that the problem requires of you. If you do have to pause and think every time you are confronted with 5 times 7, you are burdening your working memory with that task and taking up valuable space. As Willingham put it, "It is no wonder that students who have memorized math facts do better in all sorts of math tasks than students whose knowledge of math facts is absent or uncertain. And it's been shown that practicing math facts helps low-achieving students do better on more advanced mathematics" (Willingham 2009, p. 114). A similar example from my own experience involves writing students and grammar and syntax. Although you might think it's possible for students to have brilliant ideas expressed in poor grammar in a paper, in practice this almost never happens. When papers come in with really poor grammar or other mechanical problems, they almost always also contain poor or shallow thinking, lack of attention to the assignment, or major structural problems. That doesn't mean that students with poor grammar skills can't think effectively or can't also be smart. However, students who struggle with the basic requirement of putting grammatically correct sentences together have to devote their working memory space to that task and don't leave themselves space for the higher order tasks necessary to complete the assignment effectively. The student who has to think about the function of every punctuation mark isn't likely to nail the more complex task of creating an argumentative thesis. The student who has a strong mastery of grammar and mechanics, by contrast, can devote his working memory space to those more complex tasks.

The implications of this are clear enough and articulated already: whatever specific cognitive skills you want your students to develop, they should have multiple opportunities to practice beforehand. Sure, you might be thinking to yourself, but that's what homework is for! Why should I devote my valuable class time to allowing students to work on writing grammatically correct sentences or developing core math skills or answering multiple-choice questions or giving pieces of their presentations? Why can't I give them the instruction they need to practice those tasks and then send them off to complete that practice on their own? Aren't we just coddling students and wasting class time if we draw such practice activities into the classroom, even if we are doing so—as I will recommend—in the 10–15-minute periods that are the hallmark of small teaching?

To answer these questions, we have to dig a little more deeply into the idea of practice and consider the work of Harvard psychologist Ellen Langer. Decades of Langer's research on cognition and learning are distilled in a brief but wonderful book called *The Power of Mindful Learning*, which begins with a thesis that might seem in direct contradiction to Willingham's argument. "One of the most cherished myths in education or any kind of training," Langer wrote, "is that in order to learn a skill one must practice it to the point of doing it without thinking" (Langer 2007, p. 10). Doing so, she argued, leads to something called *overlearning*, which prevents us from developing and getting better at cognitive tasks: "When people overlearn a task so that they can perform it by rote, the individual steps that make up the skill come together into larger and larger units. As a consequence, the smaller components of the activity are essentially lost, yet it is by adjusting and varying those pieces that we can improve our performance" (Langer 2007, pp. 17–18).

Overlearned tasks are the ones we can perform unthinkingly and continue to perform in the same manner every time, in spite of potentially changing circumstances. Many years ago, when I first learned to ski and did so frequently, skis had the same width at the back end and the middle as they did at the front end. Fifteen years later, when I began skiing again after a long hiatus, skis had changed: now they are shaped, which means that they widen at the front and back—and that turning requires a different set of bodily movements. Even though I knew this because someone had told it to me, I couldn't figure out how to do it. I just kept doing what I had always done, fighting against the shape of my skis—not because I wasn't trying but because I couldn't understand how to move my body differently. I had overlearned my ski habits and could not adjust them to the new circumstances of my shaped skis. Langer's research suggests that the same thing can happen with the cognitive tasks we give to our students. Asking them to drill the same tasks over and over again puts them on autopilot and prevents them from refining and further developing their skills in the way that experts continually do.

To account both for the need for practice as outlined by Willingham and the desire to prevent overlearning outlined by Langer, we need to add into the mix Langer's concept of *mindful learning*. Langer defined a mindful approach to learning as having three characteristics: "the continuous creation of new categories; openness to new information; and an implicit awareness of more than one perspective" (Langer 2007, p. 4). First, the learner must be willing to shift and develop the categories that will guide her through a cognitive task. If the learner is using theory A to guide her through a problem-solving session and finds herself stuck in a dead end, she should have the ability to recognize that theory A might need modification or even need chucking out and replacing with theory B. A mindful learner cannot simply plug and chug formulae, in other words. Second, the learner must be attentive to new information that might be blocked from view by her usual approach. A rote learner will complete a task the same way every time, not noticing variations in the landscape or challenges within the problem that might help her further develop her skill levels. Finally, the mindful learner recognizes that perspectives are always limited and that final conclusions are always provisional. She accepts the possibility that new and better approaches to a problem might yet arise, and she remains open to the potential value of perspectives she doesn't inhabit. The three components of mindful learning, taken together, represent both activity and attitude: the activity involves monitoring and questioning one's approach to a routine problem or challenge; the attitude involves openness to the possibility of change.

Seen in this more full perspective, mindful learning does not necessarily conflict with the need for practice, as Willingham argued. We still want to help people develop automaticity in certain kinds of basic work to free up cognitive space for higher order cognitive tasks. However, we want them to do so consciously and with a recognition that they must pause occasionally to pull back from an automatic task and assess whether or not it's working, whether another approach might work more effectively in that moment, and how they could improve that skill. Ultimately, I did not change my ski habits until I went with a friend of mine who had undergone the same shift I had from straight to shaped skis. He pointed out several small body movements that I was doing incorrectly, so with his advice in mind I became a much more deliberate skier. I had to think more carefully about what I was doing as I carved my turns down the mountain, and I learned to pay much closer to attention to what my hips were doing, to accept feedback from my body and the terrain, and to make continual adjustments. Over time, I had to do less and less of that, as the new habits became more automatic to me. Two points remain essential, though. First, I am now a much more thoughtful skier than I ever was and enjoy the challenges of approaching and navigating different terrains in ways that I had lost when I was just thoughtlessly whizzing down the mountain. Second, even though I learned to practice more mindfully, I still had to engage in constant practice in order to master this new skill. If anything, the need for me to engage in more mindful skiing inspired me to practice even more than I otherwise would have, when I was locked into unproductive patterns.

This all sounds complex, I know. How do you help students practice enough to put some lower level skills on automatic pilot but still help them remain mindful enough to engage in occasional checking of those skills and even remain open to the possibility of doing things differently? In my skiing example, I had a friend who pointed out what I was doing wrong and who still will occasionally ski behind me and give me a pointer here and there if I ask him to. If only students had someone like that available to them—a person who could observe their practice, give them some feedback on what they were doing, and then continue to monitor their progress and remind them to remain open to other possibilities. If only ... if only ... oh, wait—that's you! Finally, we have now come around to the answer to the question you (hypothetically) posed several pages back: why can't I just provide my students with instruction and then send them off to practice on their own? Because doing so will leave them open to the possibility that they practice mindlessly, simply trying to get through their homework rather than engaging with it in the kind of thoughtful ways promoted by Langer. If you are present when they are engaged in their practice, however, you can play the role of my skiing friend: you can provide feedback while they are working, you can occasionally ask them to pause and reflect upon what they are doing (more on this next chapter), and you can offer suggestions for creative new pathways that they might try when they get stuck on a problem. You, in other words, are the best guide that students have toward mindful learning and toward practicing in ways that promote mindful learning—but you will best serve as that guide when you are present to them during their practice, whether that means standing in the room with them or interacting with them online.

Even though this still might sound like a complex task, don't overthink it (bad advice to give academics, I know). We'll get into some specific strategies in the next section. Just to demonstrate how simple it can be to help learners engage in more mindful practice, though, consider an experiment conducted by Langer and two colleagues designed to test whether they could help students learn to practice the piano mindfully. Two groups of musical novices were given some simple exercises to practice on the piano and then a 20-minute lesson on a specific piece; afterward, their playing was taped and evaluated by experts. The first group was simply instructed to do the exercises and enjoined to practice them in the traditional way: through repetition and rote learning. The second group was given this instruction:

> We would like you to try to learn these fingering exercises without relying on rote memorization. Try to keep learning new things about your piano playing. Try to change your style every few minutes, and not lock into one particular pattern. While you practice, attend to the context, which may include very subtle variations or any feelings, sensations, or thoughts you are having. (Langer 2007, p. 27)

The students in the second group were given one additional reminder about these instructions at the midway point of their practice sessions. When the two groups' playing was evaluated afterward by experts, the results confirmed the power of mindful practice: "The subjects given mindful instruction in the early steps of piano playing were rated as more competent and more creative and also expressed more enjoyment of the activity" (p. 27). If you are capable of opening your student practice sessions with instructions like the ones provided by Langer and her colleagues and of pausing students occasionally throughout the process—whether you do so individually or to the group as a whole—you are capable of helping students learn through mindful practice in your classroom.

MODELS

The models presented here will deviate slightly from the form established in the other chapters because the strategy is such a straightforward and obvious one and has been stated already: you should give students small and regular opportunities in class (or synchronously online) to practice whatever cognitive skills you would like them to develop and that they will need to succeed on your assessments. They should be able to practice these tasks in advance of and separate from formal grading, and they should receive some feedback on their practice, from you or from peers. Instead of repeating this advice in different forms, I instead outline the three steps that are essential to creating this type of practice session.

Unpack Your Assessments

Your first task is to analyze your assessments and to break them down into the various cognitive tasks that they will require of your students and to understand for yourself the priorities that you assign to those tasks when you grade the assessments. Only after you have unpacked the assessments in this way can you determine what will be most beneficial for your students to practice in class.

Once you have done this, you might find it surprising to note—as I once did—how many of the skills that you require of students on your assessments are ones you don't normally allow them to practice in your course.

For example, writing a paper of literary analysis, which most of us who teach literature ask of our students, obviously requires students to analyze and make an argument about a work of literature. That's the skill that we typically focus on in class: we model the process of analyzing literature for them, and we ask them to venture their own analyses in our class discussions or group exercises. But consider just a small number of some of the other cognitive skills that are necessary to write an effective paper of literary analysis and that would come into play in my evaluation of such a paper:

· Writing an introductory paragraph
· Crafting a one- or two-sentence argumentative thesis
· Incorporating quotations into an essay
· Building body paragraphs around evidence
· Writing according to correct grammatical conventions
· Writing a concluding paragraph

Looking over this (partial) list of skills my students would need to complete this complex assignment, I would probably pinpoint the second, third, and fourth ones as accounting for the highest proportion of the grade I will assign to their essays. In a typical class session in a literature course, I might give them some form of practice for the second skill by asking them to argue or state their positions about the work we are discussing—although even this I would typically do orally instead of in writing. However, I almost never give them time in class to develop the skill of building a paragraph around a piece of evidence or of incorporating a quotation effectively into a piece of writing.

Consider the more generic example of asking students to give a slide-based presentation: putting aside whatever cognitive tasks might be required by the specific dictates of your presentation assignment or the work of your discipline, such an assignment entails the following cognitive activities:

- Organizing material into slide-sized chunks
- Creating slides with an appropriate amount of text
- Finding, selecting, and incorporating images, video, or audio onto slides
- Balancing their spoken words with the text on the slides
- Allowing enough time for audience members to absorb the material on each slide

If you have sat through presentations at your disciplinary conferences, as I am sure most of us have, you will no doubt recognize that these are complex skills that many teachers have not yet mastered, much less students. How many times have you seen, for example, slides that are totally jam-packed with text that is then read out verbatim by the presenter? Or how many times have you seen slides that are totally jam-packed with text that are projected for less time than it would take for the audience member to read them? Did you know that research has been conducted on this very issue of whether or not we should read the text on our slides (Miller 2014, p. 154)? And if you don't specifically give students practice at creating and speaking from slides—based either on that research or on your own experience as a deliverer of presentations or as someone who has witnessed many of them—how are you expecting your students to do it effectively? And how fair is it to grade them on it?

I know that a common (if unspoken) objection to this line of thinking might be that the students should have learned and have practiced these skills somewhere else: in their composition courses, or in a speech class, or in high school, or in someone else's class. Maybe. But unless your students are walking into your class and nailing their presentations from day one, they obviously still need practice at it. If you are not going to give them that practice, whom do you expect to do it?

First step: break down your major assessments as finely as you can, and identify the cognitive skills that students would need to succeed on that assessment.

Parcel Them Out and Practice Them

Second step: create small teaching opportunities for your students to practice them in class or online.

Practice strikes me as an especially appropriate activity to assign to the closing 10–15 minutes of class, as your practice session can help the students work on skills that stem from that day's class material. If we are having an open-ended discussion about a poem in my literature course, in which both I and the students have articulated various thesis-type ideas about what we think the poem means, I could close that discussion 10 minutes before the end of class and ask students to write two sample thesis statements in their notebooks about the poem based on the arguments they heard that day. Even better, I could close the class 15 minutes early, spend 5 minutes reviewing with them the components that make for an effective argumentative thesis, and *then* ask them to take 10 minutes and write two sample thesis statements. At the beginning of the next class session, before we moved onto new material, I might ask them to select one of the two thesis statements they crafted, find a quote from the poem that would support it, and then write a single body paragraph centered on that quote. (Again, ideally, I would perhaps spend just a couple of minutes beforehand reminding them about the essential components of a good body paragraph.) Giving students a dozen such in-class tasks over the course of the semester would provide them with substantial practice at skills they need for many types of college essay assignments.

For a presentation assignment, you might pick a day 2 weeks in advance of the actual presentations and ask students to bring their laptops to class. In the final 10 minutes of a class in which you present some new material to them, ask them to pair up and work together on the creation of a single slide designed to teach an audience about Concept A. In the following class sessions, allot the final 10 minutes of each class to asking a handful of students to stand up and give a 2-minute presentation of the slide they created. Better yet, as in the writing example, make it the final 15 minutes and spend the first 5 of those reminding them that reading text directly from slides can produce something called the *redundancy effect*, which can reduce learning, but that too much difference between what's on the slide and what they say also has been shown to reduce learning. So they should be searching for what Michelle Miller described as the "'Goldilocks' principle with respect to the discrepancy between the narration and the visually presented slide"—they should clearly reference and highlight the key components of what they have put on the slide, but not simply read it out directly (Miller 2014, p. 154). Giving students the opportunity to create several practice slides and then to work on speaking those slides to an audience would go a long way toward improving the majority of student presentations I have seen.

Provide Feedback

Third step: provide feedback on their practice efforts.

The ideal practice–feedback situation is something like what I experienced with my more experienced skiing friend—while

I practiced, he observed and offered timely suggestions on how to improve. This kind of feedback can occur in individual tutoring sessions, in sports coaching of many kinds, and in arts instruction—think of a student practicing the piano under the watchful eye of her instructor. Although we obviously can't create this kind of one-on-one feedback loop in our typical college courses, we still should search for ways to provide students with feedback on their practice. The simplest means of doing so, in a face-to-face classroom, is to combine individual and group feedback during and after the practice session. While students are engaged in their practice work, circulate among them and offer individual feedback on the work of as many students as you can. You will probably find that patterns of problems begin to emerge as you observe the work of more and more students. After you have offered some individual feedback, then, you can pause the session and offer feedback on those common issues to the entire group. This process can be repeated as often as necessary. At the start of such a practice session, you will have to make clear that you intend to provide feedback in this manner. If you don't, you might find that some students feel uncomfortable at receiving feedback in this way, thinking that you are singling them out for some reason. Just announce at the start of your first session that you will be circulating and offering feedback to as many students as you can and using what you observe to help the entire group.

Obviously you can do the same thing in online environments, offering individualized or spot feedback on practice work and then using what you observed to offer more general remarks to the whole class. If you do use this method to offer feedback, either face-to-face or online, it's worth a few minutes of reflection on how you can spread the individualized feedback around the entire room so that as many people as possible receive individualized attention over the course of the whole semester. You can use the shape of the room, the rows or columns of desks, or even the course roster to help ensure you are circulating among the students in an equitable way.

Finally, although much of the feedback you give to students might offer simple tweaks or tips on how to accomplish a particular task more effectively, you can certainly shape that feedback so that it pushes students toward the kind of mindful learning Langer advocates. In the provocative closing chapters of *The Power of Mindful Learning,* she made the case that the kind of open-ended, flexible thinking fostered by mindful learning constitutes the very heart of what we think about as intelligence:

> Although flexible thinking is the essence of mindfulness, flexibility can also be considered a quality of intelligent thinking. We all have a repertoire of lower-level procedures and higher-level strategies that may be tried in novel settings. The larger our repertoire and the less we are attached to any specific procedure or strategy, the more flexible our thinking is likely to be … Our general capacity to sort through these various strategies and procedures and assess which can be applied most appropriately to a novel task is the process usually called intelligent thinking. (p. 113)

In other words, intelligence in the completion of cognitive tasks consists of the ability to step back from our familiar patterns, consider whether alternatives exist, and then recognize whether any of those alternatives might work more effectively. So if we want students to think in these intelligent and creative ways about the cognitive tasks required by our assessments, we should encourage them to do so in our practice sessions. Feedback might occasionally nudge them to step back from the specific task and consider alternatives. Why have you chosen to use that strategy for your introduction? What alternatives might you have chosen? Is that the only formula that you could have used to solve this problem? Have you ever encountered a question like this outside of this course? How did you answer it then? If I posed this question to someone who had not taken this course, how do you think they would go about trying to answer it? Questions like these, designed to push thinkers up to a more aerial view of their practice, may help create the kind of mindful learners that don't lock into familiar patterns and rely on rote repetition to complete their cognitive tasks.

PRINCIPLES

As Ellen Langer's theory of mindful learning reminds us, not all practice is alike. But any opportunity you give your students to practice cognitive activities in your classroom will likely yield them benefits when they are faced with completing your assessments. Keep in mind the following principles as you reflect on how to incorporate effective practice sessions into your course.

Make Time for In-Class Practice While you certainly can and should give students practice opportunities through homework, make time for it in your classroom or (for online courses) synchronous sessions. Practice that takes place away from the presence of an instructor can become a breeding ground for overlearning, mindless repetition, and the development of wrong or poor habits. Practice that takes place with the benefit of your presence and feedback has potential to create more powerful learning. Keeping the sessions small will help you find space for them in your valuable classroom time.

Space It Out According to the research we reviewed on spacing and interleaving, five 10-minute practice sessions spaced out throughout the a course will work more effectively than a single

50-minute practice session. This makes practicing according to the small teaching paradigm ideal for learning: the multiple, brief sessions a small teaching approach would recommend are exactly what should benefit your students most fully.

Practice Mindfully Repetition helps us master cognitive tasks in the same way that it helps us master shooting free throws in basketball, skiing on shaped skis, or speaking confidently in front of an audience. Although repetition on its own will produce a certain base level of competency, it won't help us grow and improve unless we pause at least occasionally to reflect on what we are doing, why we are doing it, and whether alternative pathways might exist. Use practice sessions to nudge students toward mindful learning.

SMALL TEACHING QUICK TIPS: PRACTICE

Much of the work of this small teaching technique happens outside of the classroom, as you analyze the assessments you give and break them down into their component skill parts. Once you have done that, make a little space in class for each of them and guide your students toward mindful learning.

- Before the semester begins, brainstorm a comprehensive list of cognitive skills your students will need to develop to succeed in your course.
- Prioritize them; decide which ones students will need to develop most immediately and which ones can emerge only after they have developed some basic skills.
- Review your course schedule and decide where you can make space for small practice sessions in key skills prior to your major assessments; mark those sessions on the syllabus schedule.

- Stick to your plan. Prior to any major assessment, ensure that students have had multiple opportunities to practice the skills they will need to do well, from creating slides or writing paragraphs to answering multiple-choice questions.

CONCLUSION

As you can probably tell from the examples I gave throughout this chapter, incorporating brief practice sessions into the classroom has been one of the most important changes I have made to my teaching in recent years. After the success I had in helping students give more effective presentations, I began moving more and more skill-based activities into the classroom, including everything from writing introductory paragraphs to writing sample essay exam questions. All of that practice, along with the positive effects that appeared in the work of my students, convinced me completely of its potential to improve student learning and performance.

I can't close this chapter without noting one hurdle that I had to overcome as I gradually shifted more and more practice sessions into my classroom: the uneasy feeling I would get when students were working away at some task and I wasn't actively engaged in what I had always thought about as teaching. I wasn't lecturing to them, or leading a discussion, or trying to keep a handle on a group project, or supervising an assessment. These are comfortable and familiar activities for teachers; observing, listening, and reflecting seem less familiar to us in the classroom. However, if you can learn to use the time in which they are practicing as an opportunity for you to gain a better understanding of their current skill levels and can offer them both individualized and group feedback, you will grow more accustomed to those moments in which you are not teaching in more familiar ways, just as your students will grow more accustomed to thinking about the classroom space not as a place to sit passively and absorb material but as a site in which to engage in active, mindful practice of important intellectual skills.

Chapter 6

Self-Explaining

INTRODUCTION

I suspect you could theoretically survive parenting a child without ever raising your voice in anger—an achievement I certainly can't claim to have made. All the restraint you may have demonstrated in the early years of parenting, however, will melt when your child begins learning to drive, and you find yourself in the passenger seat of a terrifying death machine with a 16-year-old at the helm. No matter how carefully they have studied the rules of the road and practiced in parking lots, 16-year-olds who are learning to drive do things like ignore yield signs or forget to look in both directions before pulling out into traffic. At those moments you can choose either to raise your voice or to crash.

I have chosen to raise my voice.

However justified I may feel in barking an emergency instruction in potentially hazardous driving situations, my 16-year-old daughter does not seem to appreciate the value of what I am doing for us both (i.e., saving our lives). This means that driving lessons, which I have just recently completed with my second child, consist of tension-filled rides around the neighborhood in which I am continually on the verge of a panic attack and she is continually on the verge of tears. During the time when I was supervising these white-knuckled drives, I also happened to be doing some reading about self-explanation and learning, the basic premise of which is that *learners benefit from explaining out loud (to themselves or others) what they are doing during the completion of a learning task.* Less to improve her learning than to diffuse the tension in the car, I began asking my daughter to tell me about what she was doing as she drove. One of her problems had been that she tended to drive too close to the right side of the road, perhaps out of an exaggerated (and understandable) concern for not drifting into oncoming traffic. When I asked her to talk about what she was doing as she drove, she noticed this issue herself, about which I had reminded her earlier (like a thousand times), and she made a self-correction. She navigated more to the center of the road. This happened several other times with other driving tasks. Whenever I asked her to explain what she was doing, she would analyze her own driving in ways that didn't seem to happen when she was just sitting there attempting to navigate the road and waiting for me to shout at her. It's a strategy I won't soon forget, since I still have three more children who will turn 16 sometime in the not-too-distant future.

This helpful incident was my first real observation of the power of self-explanation, a learning strategy that can assist students who are attempting to master a cognitive skill. As we saw in the last chapter, the absolutely most helpful thing that learners need to do to master a skill is to practice it as frequently as possible. For this reason novice drivers like my daughter are required by my state to have 40 hours of practice behind the wheel between the time they get their learner's permit and the time that they can apply for a driver's license. Nothing substitutes for hours and hours behind the wheel, but we saw in the second half of the last chapter the importance of practicing mindfully, of stepping away from rote exercises as frequently as possible to monitor one's performance, to seek opportunities for improvement, and to explore alternative strategies or perspectives. Instructors can play an essential role in nudging learners toward this mindful learning when they are present at skill-based practice sessions. Self-explanation represents one very simple technique for fostering mindful learning during skill-based practice, but it also can help improve comprehension by requiring learners to make connections between their knowledge and their skills. The best self-explanation techniques prompt learners to articulate not only what they are doing but also *why* they are doing it, and that second requirement helps ensure that students can't simply connect the dots to make a picture: they must tie their doing to their knowing. As such, it has the power to draw together the aims of the previous two chapters in this part—and can do so in the kinds of easy, simple-to-use exercises that are the hallmark of small teaching.

IN THEORY

The first major study to demonstrate that self-explanations can support learning did so in an effort to analyze how students learned from worked examples—in other words, from sample problems that had been worked out in advance and then were reviewed step by step for the benefit of the students (Chi, Bassok, Lewis, Reimann, and Glaser 1989). In tackling this issue, this study explored a fundamental paradox at the heart of learning from examples more generally. Plenty of research demonstrates that students benefit from the use of examples in learning rather than simply being presented with theories or ideas or principles. An equally robust body of literature also demonstrates that students who learn from examples often have trouble transferring their knowledge acquired from examples to new contexts. This problem becomes especially acute when learners are attempting to use knowledge gained from examples to solve new problems. As the authors of the study explain, "students who have studied examples often cannot solve problems that require a very slight deviation from the example solution" (Chi, Bassok, Lewis, Reimann, and Glaser 1989, p. 148). Although studying worked-out examples can help students solve future problems that are *isomorphic* (i.e., taking the same form as the original problem), doing so often does not translate well into helping students solve problems that require *far transfer* (carrying principles or theories from the initial context to a completely new context). The researchers in this case, led by Michelene T. H. Chi, argued that worked-out examples often elide steps or fail to articulate conditions that are important for the learner to understand. To help them fill in those gaps, they hypothesized that learners who self-explain while they are studying worked examples—doing things like monitoring their comprehension, or paraphrasing the textbook, or stating the relevant principles out loud—would improve their ability to solve future problems.

Their experiment consisted of two phases: a first one in which their subjects studied a series of worked-out examples from a physics textbook and answered questions to test their declarative knowledge; and a second phase in which they were asked to solve problems based on that knowledge. In this experiment the researchers did not so much prompt self-explanation as listen for it; they wanted to see if differences in understanding and problem solving would be tied to spontaneous self-explanations generated by the learners. The subject size was small, just 10 students, who were ultimately divided into two groups: *Good* and *Poor*. The Good students had a mean success rate of 82 percent on the problems, whereas the Poor students came in at 46 percent (p. 158). The difference in the amount of self-explanations generated by the two groups is startling: Good students offered around 140 lines of self-explanation in the transcripts, whereas Poor students generated only around 20 (p. 159). Not wanting to rely simply on volume of words, though, the researchers looked more carefully at the self-explanation transcripts and eliminated less relevant comments to tabulate only those that connected to the major ideas of the subject matter. The differences narrowed but remained quite strong: 51 for the Good students versus 18 for the Poor (p. 159). The really astonishing point about these results is that the first phase of the study showed almost no differences between the Good and Poor students in terms of their declarative knowledge of the physics principles in question. In other words, all students could score equally well when they were asked to do things like provide definitions; the stark differences between the two only emerged when they had to apply their declarative knowledge to solving problems.

When they explored what types of comments the Good learners actually made during their self-explanations, they found three basic categories of material. First, and most important, the Good learners generated *explanations*. As they described such statements, "Explanations consist of inferences about the conditions, the consequences, the goals, and the meaning of various mathematical actions described in the example. Furthermore, a large number of explanations that the Good students provided were judged to be guided by the principles, concepts, and definitions introduced in the text" (p. 169). Good learners, in other words, made explanatory statements that tied specific problems to general principles; they connected knowing and doing. Second, the Good learners frequently *monitored comprehension*. In other words, they stated whether or not they understood what they were reading and were not shy about admitting when they were stuck. "Good students," they suggested, "realize that they do not understand more often than the Poor students" (p. 172). Most important, when the Good students recognized and articulated gaps in their understanding, they sought to correct them. The final category included all other types of substantive statements the students might have made, including *paraphrasing*. Good students restated different aspects of the problems in their own words. In all of these areas, the researchers ultimately argue, the Good students were improving their problem-solving abilities and were linking their knowledge to problem-solving skills by creating what they call "inference rules" (p. 177). By this they mean that learners are gaining a clearer understanding of how to apply principles within different contexts. Inference rules "spell out more clearly the specific conditions or situations in which a specific action is to be taken" (p. 178), which helps learners recognize when learned principles might apply to novel contexts.

Ultimately, the authors of this study concluded that "self explanations not only construct better problem-solving procedures, but they also help students to understand the underlying principles more completely" (p. 169). This study was incomplete in that it relied on the students to generate those self-explanations, which would have limited use for us as college and university instructors. Obviously we could advise students to engage in self-explanations while they are studying examples in our textbooks, but we advise students to do lots of things, many of which they ignore. The question then arises as to whether self-explanations generated in response to prompts from a teacher would have the same effect as self-explanations spontaneously generated by the students. It may certainly be the case, after all, that self-explanations worked for the Good students in Chi et al.'s initial study because those Good students were good students and self-explanation was simply one of a package of activities in which they engaged that helped them learn. However, if you isolate the single activity of self-explanation and require students of all levels to employ it in their learning activities, will it still have the same powerful effect that it had in this original study?

This was the question that Chi and another set of colleagues asked and answered in a second experiment conducted several years later with another group of students, this time shifting the content from problem solving in physics to understanding the circulatory system in the human body. The purpose of this revisitation of the self-explanation effect, they explained, was to extend it "from skill acquisition to the learning of a coherent body of new knowledge" and to see whether "the beneficial effect of self-explanations can be achieved merely by prompting students to self-explain" (Chi, DeLeeuw, Chiu, LaVancher 1984, p. 442). This study has the greatest implications for us as instructors because—if prompting self-explanation demonstrates the same powerful learning effects as spontaneously generated self-explanation—it gives us the opportunity to incorporate it into our teaching practices. Unfortunately, this study shifts us away from college-level students, but it does so as a part of a larger effort by the authors to test the extent to which the positive learning effects of self-explanation identified in the first study would appear under an entirely different set of conditions. In this second study, they worked with a new age group (eighth graders), a new discipline (biology), and a new type of learning (text comprehension versus problem solving), and they prompted self-explanations rather than simply observing students generating them spontaneously. They make a good argument that these represent such a complete set of differences from the first study that if they observe the same learning effects, self-explanation has powerful potential as a teaching strategy for instructors at all levels.

In the study, eighth graders were asked to read brief passages from a high school biology textbook about the human circulatory system and were prompted to self-explain what they were learning after each sentence they read. A second group of eighth graders were asked to read the same passages from the textbook twice but without self-explanation prompts. (This second reading ensured that they spent equal amounts of time on the text as the self-explaining students.) The students who were prompted to self-explain did so in three ways: they were instructed in advance to self-explain after they read each of the 101 sentences of the passage; every few sentences they were prompted to answer a question about the *function* of the circulatory system part they were learning about (i.e., what is the function of the septum?); they were occasionally asked by the researchers to clarify or elaborate on their initial self-explanations. Both sets of students were given pretests on the circulatory system and then tested a week after their study sessions. In these final tests, students were asked multiple types of questions about the material they read: some required memorization of basic information about the circulatory system (i.e., "What does hemoglobin transport?"), and others required them to make inferences about the system based on what they had learned ("Why doesn't the pulmonary vein have a valve in it?"). A final category of questions required them to make even more complex inferences about the implications of the circulatory system for human health (such as how the circulatory system would account for the effects of a poisonous snake bite). This range of questions seems to mimic what students typically find on exams in higher education, testing students on both memorization and more complex critical thinking skills (p. 448).

The study results confirm the findings of the first experiment. The self-explanation prompted students experienced a 32 percent gain in their knowledge of the circulatory system from the pretest to the posttest, whereas the unprompted students experienced a 22 percent gain (p. 453). Parsing the results a little more finely, Chi and colleagues noticed that the improvement was slightly more extensive on the more complex questions. In the third and fourth question categories, the prompted students improved 22 percent from pretest to posttest, whereas the unprompted students improved only 12 percent (p. 453). The study also looked at the volume of self-explanations offered by those in the prompted group, separating them out into high and low self-explainers. Even in this more finely tuned analysis, the differences persisted.

Analyzing both self-generated drawings made by the students and their verbal explanations to see how they reflected an accurate mental model of the circulatory system, they found that the high self-explainers were much more likely to develop such an accurate model than the low self-explainers. "Eliciting self-explanations," they conclude, "clearly enhances learning and understanding of a coherent body of new knowledge, whether one compares the amount learned by the prompted and unprompted students, or whether one compares the amount learned by the high and low self-explainers" (p. 469). Good students, in other words, may naturally self-explain more than weaker students; however, we can still help those weaker students by prompting self-explanations.

Before shifting to our models, consider one final and more recent study on the role of self-explanation, this one working with students who were learning how to solve probability problems in statistics in an online environment. The researchers had students review worked examples and then solve a succession of problems online, some of which included prompts for self-explanation and some of which did not. In the self-explanation condition, "the learner was encouraged to self-explain each solved solution step by first examining the step and then identifying which principle of probability the step exemplified" (Atkinson, Merrill, and Renkl 2003, p. 777). This meant literally that the learner saw, prior to her attempt to resolve each new step of the solution, a drop-down menu containing several possible principles that might be relevant for that step and that she had to select one of them before proceeding. It's worth noting what a weak form of self-explanation this is: simply prompting learners to stop and select the relevant principle rather than requiring them to articulate it themselves. Yet, in spite of the very diluted form of self-explanation in which these learners engaged, the positive learning effects appeared strongly in the students' ability to solve problems on a posttest in both near-transfer problems (ones similar to ones they had just studied) and far-transfer problems (ones that stemmed from similar principles but had few similar surface features). The researchers noted in their discussion that the students received immediate feedback on their selection of the principle, and they theorized that this might be a crucial step—a point worth mentioning in considering how to translate self-explanation into small teaching activities. Overall, though, the study confirms Chi et al.'s findings that self-explaining while learning to solve problems, even in modest ways, can provide a significant learning boost. We are left, then, with only one final question: Why does self-explanation work?

Chi and her colleagues theorized in the first study that self-explanation may benefit learning because worked examples can never fully explain *every* step necessary to the solving of a problem. Some steps are taken for granted, whereas others might make sense only to those who have certain background or contextual knowledge in place already. Self-explanation enables learners to fill in the gaps of these unarticulated steps when they are studying worked examples; without a grasp of those unartic-ulated steps, which help provide a fuller understanding of the problem's condition and contexts, they are less able to generalize from a worked example to a new problem. Likewise, in the second study, the authors suggested again that textbooks leave gaps in their explanations, requiring the contribution of the learner: "Any expository passage leaves a great deal of room for readers to provide their own inferences to bridge the gaps in the information provided. Hence, self-explaining seems to be a necessary activity in order to maximize what is learned from any expository passage" (Chi, DeLeeuw, Chiu, and LaVancher 1984, p. 445). The first study referred to the power of self-explanation in helping students develop unstated inference rules; here they seem to speak more generally about the kinds of inferences we must make on first exposure to any new knowledge domain. This explanation seems analogous to the theory of reader-response criticism in literary studies, which has long argued that reading any complex sentence entails a continuous process of filling gaps, making inferences, and supplying relevant context. Chi et al.'s theories are making a similar claim for exposure to new knowledge more generally, whether that takes the form of reading or learning to solve problems. The important takeaway from both studies is that self-explanation can prove to be a vital tool in helping learners fill gaps and make inferences in learning-productive ways.

A second explanation for the power of self-explanation is that it helps learners modify and improve their existing perceptions or knowledge of a subject matter. One of Chi's most recent contributions to the literature is a co-authored survey of much of the research that has been conducted thus far on self-explanation in education. As that article explained, "Learners can come in [to a class or new discipline] with their own ideas, or their own mental models of a concept. These mental models are typically flawed. When a learner encounters instructional material that conflicts with their existing mental models, self-explaining helps repair and revise their understanding" (Chiu and Chi 2014, p. 92). As Chapter 4 noted, some fascinating research in physics has demonstrated how learners can sometimes hold contradictory concepts in a field without ever recognizing or fixing their understanding. It may be that the gap between their existing knowledge and what they learn is too wide and that they can't see their way from one side to the other. Effective self-explanation prompts can provide the tools that help students recognize the problems with their current understanding and point them to the principles or steps that will lead them to new understanding. Ultimately, for both of these explanations for the learning power of self-explanation, it seems clear that monitoring comprehension plays a key role. Self-explanation helps learners recognize problems in their understanding—whether those problems are gaps in their knowledge or mistaken theories or ideas—and prompts them to take productive steps forward in their thinking.

MODELS

Much of the research that presents methods for improving student learning through self-explanation focuses on training students to self-explain during their study behaviors. This seems to me like a valuable approach to recommend to students or implement in tutoring or supervised study sessions, but consider these models for incorporating self-explanation into your courses through small teaching activities.

Select the Principle

Remember that one of the studies supporting the power of self-explanation involved learners selecting a principle from a drop-down menu before solving a problem (Atkinson, Renkl, and Merrill 2003). Those of you who teach in science, technology, engineering, and mathematics (STEM) disciplines and assign homework problems online or teach online might use this study as an incentive to create or seek out learning management systems or programs that enable or require students to pause at key points during their problem-solving sessions and identify the underlying principle that will guide their next step. This strategy might work because the continuous pausing to reflect on principles while solving a problem could eventually create a mental habit that prompts students to engage in such reflection whenever they are faced with the challenge of solving a problem. The other learning strategy tested in that same study was something called *backward fading*, in which students were simply observing or reviewing in the first worked-out examples they encountered; in the next set of examples, they had to complete one or two steps on their own; in the next set, they completed still more of the steps; and so on until they were completing the problem on their own. The researchers found that self-explanation combined with backward fading produced especially robust learning, so it might be the case that self-explanation prompts prove most strong for new learners and that they become less important as learners develop the habit of stopping to reflect on principles on their own and don't require the prompts anymore. In this case, as with many of the techniques discussed in this book, the small teaching strategy of prompting students to select the principle they are using to solve problems online will likely offer the strongest benefit to new learners in a field and to lower performing students more generally.

One important caveat here is that this article notes a previous study in which learners had to *generate* the principles rather than *selecting* them, and in that study self-explanation did not improve learning. The researchers in the current study theorize that the learners in that previous study had too many demands made on their working memory in the tasks they were assigned (giving the self-explanation in that earlier study required the learner to complete several steps on the computer). The more simple opportunity to view several choices and select the correct principle from a drop-down menu made less demands on their working memory, enabling them to concentrate on the problem while still prompting them to tie their cognitive activity with a principle they had learned. So it may be that your first efforts with small teaching forms of self-explanation should begin with pointing students to possible principles and asking them to choose. This seems like an easy tweak that can be made to any virtual learning environment featuring problem solving, but it could just as easily appear in a face-to-face environment in which students are solving problems. Say you are giving your students 10 minutes at the end of a class to solve a type of math problem that you have demonstrated in class that day. As they begin their work, write down three or four possible theorems or principles on the board, and ask them to note in the margin of their paper, as they complete their work, where the relevant principles on the board came into play while they were completing their solutions. For online or traditional homework, make sure they can see the possible principles at the top of the page, and require them, in the same way, to note the application of relevant principles at key junctures along the way. However you need to adapt it to your specific course, the small teaching strategy here entails requiring students who are solving problems to consider a list of possible principles that will guide their work and occasionally to pause and identify the principle that will determine their next step.

Why Are You Doing That?

Most of the work on self-explanation has been conducted on helping students develop their problem-solving abilities, which means most of the research had been conducted in STEM disciplines since they typically assess understanding through the use of problems. The recommendation I am about to make represents an effort to apply the principle of self-explanation to other kinds of disciplines, but you should note that it does not enjoy the more specific support from the learning research that self-explanation in STEM disciplines does. Nevertheless, the work we ask students to complete in writing papers, preparing presentations, and creating other kinds of large-scale assignments could be considered a form of problem solving or at least as a process analogous to problem solving. If we think about these tasks in that way, then self-explanation could play a helpful role here as well. There are lots of good reasons to ask students to break down larger projects like papers and presentations into smaller chunks and complete them over several weeks, one of which is that it helps students stay on task. As I argued elsewhere, it can also help ensure that students do not engage in academic dishonesty by allowing you to get glimpses of their work as it proceeds, thereby preventing them from purchasing some work wholesale and skipping required steps along the way (Lang 2013).

As we saw in the previous chapter, giving students brief periods of time in class to practice the skills they will need for their papers or projects constitutes one highly recommended small teaching strategy. The possibility of students learning from self-explanation offers another excellent reason to parcel out the tasks of larger projects like papers or presentations. Assume your students have a paper due in 3 weeks that requires them to make use of four or five specific writing or analytic skills you have worked on in class. You might allow the final 10–15 minutes of one class per week for students to do some drafting of those essays, informed by the lessons of that specific class period and focused on a specific step in the paper-writing process. One such brief session might be reserved, for example, for drafting an opening paragraph designed to grab the attention of the reader and entice her to keep reading. While the students complete this work, you can walk around and prompt individual students with some form of a very simple question: "Why are you doing that?" In other words, what introduction-writing principle are you using here? Playing on the reader's emotions? Surprising the reader with a shocking statistic? Seeking to find common ground with the reader? Asking the student to pause and articulate the reason for her writing choices should help tap into the learning power of self-explanation. As she explains her choices, she might recognize how to improve what she is doing—just as my daughter learned to correct her driving simply by explaining aloud what she was doing on the road. This general approach—pausing students who are working and prompting them to explain the principle or reason for a choice they are making—could help any time students are working in class, but it seems to me like it would be particularly helpful when students are moving toward paper or project assignments. I know from my own experience teaching writing that students need frequent reminders to apply the principles that we have observed in other writers to their own compositions; in-class writing sessions provide me with a great opportunity to push them back to the principles and deploy them in their writing. So the simple small teaching strategy here consists of pausing working students now and again to ask them to explain what they are doing.

You could just as easily require this of students who are completing projects online. For example, say you are asking students to put together a presentation for an online course you are teaching. Assume as well that you have taught them a few things about how to give presentations, such as how to combine text and graphics in ways that are visually appealing or how to ensure that slides are not overly busy with text or are clearly organized. Instead of simply asking the students to turn in the final presentation, ask them to select any three slides and write an explanation for their design choice in the notes section of those slides. What strategy for creating effective presentations did you use, you might ask them, in constructing and organizing these specific slides? Again, the hope here would be that the students who have to articulate their design strategy for three slides will learn to think about and apply that design strategy to all of the slides they are creating.

Peer Instruction

The use of peer instruction, a teaching strategy made famous by Harvard physicist Eric Mazur, offers a great opportunity to incorporate small teaching self-explanations into a class, especially larger lecture-style courses. More than 20 years ago, Mazur helped develop clickers as a teaching technology to support the process of students learning from one another in his courses. What he labeled as peer instruction process can take a variety of forms, but the basic model looks like this (Schell 2012):

1. The instructor poses or projects on the classroom screen a question that requires thinking or problem-solving skills.
2. The students take a minute or two to attempt to solve the problem or answer the question on their own and to record their answer with their clickers or other personal response system technology (even colored index cards will work for this purpose). Answers are immediately visible to the instructor.
3. The students then are asked to take a few minutes to turn to a neighbor and justify or explain their answer.
4. The students then resubmit their answers, which again are immediately visible to the instructor.
5. The instructor asks a few students to provide their explanations for their answers and provides the correct answer.

After this final step, the instructor has a variety of options available to her. If most of the students answered the question correctly the second time and the explanations elicited from a handful of students seem to be on target, she can move forward to the next course topic. If, however, the answers from the class are mostly incorrect or the student explanations seem confused, she can pause and revisit the topic that has been under review and then undertake the process again. Derek Bruff's *Teaching with Classroom Response Systems* offers an excellent guide for instructors interested in exploring this teaching format in greater depth (Bruff 2009).

I know that some instructors who use clickers only follow the first three steps, which is absolutely fine. Even by posing questions in the middle of a class, soliciting the answers of every student, and then gauging new instruction accordingly you are injecting an element of active learning into the class that surely has some value. This obviously does not count as peer instruction, though, since no peer instruction happens in that model. If you want to add the learning benefits of self-explanation to your clicker classes and truly engage in peer instruction, you have to incorporate that key fourth step. In a brief video that was made about Mazur's use of this teaching method, which you can find online at the *Turn to Your Neighbor* peer instruction blog from Mazur's research group, the camera holds for a few moments on a group of students who are engaged in that fourth step. One of the students offers her answer to the question, and a student with a puzzled look on his face says in response: "How do you know that?" (Schell 2012). The student who must respond to that question has to engage in a form of self-explanation—and hence should benefit from the positive learning effect that has been described in this chapter. It would be a simple enough effort to enhance learning from self-explanation during peer instruction by always nudging students to refer to the principles that guided their responses when they are explaining their answers to their peers. In some cases, as with the previously described computer-aided self-explanation prompts, you might even show a list of possible principles on the projector screen after the students have made their first answer and prompt them to select which principles led them to that first answer—and which one now seems correct to them.

Think Aloud

Theorists in nursing education have written about an approach to helping students develop clinical reasoning skills that strikes me as offering similar benefits to the peer instruction techniques Mazur developed (Banning 2004). The think-aloud technique of working with nursing students asks them simply to speak out their reasoning as they are attempting to make clinical diagnoses—a consummate form of self-explanation. One overview of the think-aloud approach in nursing education describes its benefits in ways that parallel the benefits of peer instruction. In the same way that the teacher in a peer instruction session gains access to the thought processes of his students, so the think-aloud approach can "provide insights into the types of question(s) that are asked, the train of thought, the ability to make connections and form bridges between core concepts and peripheral subjects, the use of prior knowledge and experiential learning to problem solve and the assessment of the challenges and difficulties encountered during reasoning" (Banning 2004, p. 10). Nursing students who are thinking aloud in class or on rounds can benefit not only from the consequent suggestions or corrections of the instructor but also from their fellow students—another shared feature with peer instruction. Instructors who teach in fields in which students are frequently working individually on developing specific skills (e.g., performing arts, mechanics of various kinds) can layer self-explanation on to the work of their students at any time, as can teachers who are having students doing in-class experiments or laboratory work. Institute a schedule of regular small opportunities for students to pause and self-explain while they work. Consider the think-aloud as another potential way to frame the activity of asking students to explain their reasoning, problem solving, or other cognitive work to each other or to you to help them both connect to principles and allow you both to better understand where they still need help.

Finally, you might consider students who visit you in office hours as ripe candidates for self-explanatory learning. When a student wants help with a paper or project or concept in your office hours, keep this research in mind and prompt the students to self-explain as much as possible, rather than simply reviewing the correct answers or strategies for them.

PRINCIPLES

Self-explanation is one of the least studied teaching activities covered in this book, which gives you more room to experiment but also more opportunities to wander away from what has been clearly established in the research. Keep these three principles in mind as you reflect on how or whether self-explanation belongs in your classroom.

Scaffold Self-Explanation Self-explanation is a complex cognitive activity in its own right, one in which the learner must engage while doing something else. Some research on self-explanation has demonstrated little or no gains in learning, and one theory about those experiments has been that the self-explanation requirement can actually interfere with early-stage learning. So consider how you can scaffold self-explanation requirements to account for this. Initially you might offer students simple choices in selecting possible principles to apply in their work; as they become more skilled, you might ask them to generate their own self-explanations. Don't overtax those working memories.

Point to Principles Although a variety of possible explanations for the power of self-explanations exist, some of which have been referenced already, the most convincing one to me is that self-explanations in problem solving help students connect theory with practice, or principles with concrete steps, or knowledge with doing. But just as we saw with the theory of connections, which the instructor can facilitate but the student must ultimately make, you can provide lots of examples of how principles appear in practice but ultimately the students have to draw these two components together themselves. Consider, then, how you can create opportunities for self-explanation that require students to select or articulate principles as they are making choices, searching for solutions, or revising their work.

Utilize Peer Power Envisioning how to solicit self-explanations from a class of 20 students, much less a class of 200, can be a daunting task. So don't neglect the fact that the room (whether real or virtual) contains lots of other potential listeners for student self-explanations. Whether you use the formal peer instruction process developed by Eric Mazur, the think-aloud approach of nursing education, or some other approach of your own devising, consider whether some student self-explanations can be directed at peers as well as for your benefit. At times it might be more helpful for students to offer their self-explanations to another novice learner, who can better understand their difficulties, than it would be for them to articulate them to you. Remember, though, that self-explanations will be most helpful when the learners receive feedback on their work—so you still might follow up peer activities with a large-group session in which you solicit some explanations and can provide a response.

SMALL TEACHING QUICK TIPS: SELF-EXPLAINING

Self-explanations can happen when students are doing cognitive work of any kind, and offer an excellent route to the kind of mindful learning described in the last chapter. Put in practice in the office, in the classroom, and on the course website.

- For online homework or readings, create spaces for students to self-explain while they work; for newer learners in a field, use drop-down menus that require them to select principles or theories rather than asking them to generate them on their own.
- When students are solving problems at the board, doing laboratory work, or preparing performances, create a regular schedule of opportunities or requirements for them to self-explain their process.

- Use peer instruction with personal response systems and three key steps: students provide an answer, pause and explain it to their neighbors, and then revise their answers.
- Allow class time for students to practice the skills they will need to succeed in assessed activities (as outlined in the previous chapter), and circulate and prompt self-explanations individually while they work.
- In all forms of self-explanation prompts, push students to tie their knowledge of information, principles, theories, and formulae to the specific task they are completing.

CONCLUSION

In that recent summary article surveying the research on self-explanation, Chiu and Chi (2014) pointed out that the research on which types of learners benefit most from self-explanation has yielded decidedly mixed results:

> Self-explanation has been found to be beneficial for low-knowledge students ... or students with no prior knowledge of the subject ... Some researchers suggest that there may be a greater benefit of self-explanations with more knowledge to draw upon ... Many studies find self-explanation beneficial regardless of prior knowledge ... The lack of a clear trend in these studies indicates that self-explanations can benefit students with different abilities in different ways. (p. 95)

As the research on self-explanation continues to evolve, undoubtedly underlying principles or nuances will emerge that account for the differences in these findings, and help provide more specific suggestions for effective implementation. But don't let the lack of perfect evidence here become the enemy of the good.

As Chiu and Chi also discussed, the real benefit of self-explanation is that it provides another opportunity for instructors to foster active engagement in their students: "Self-explaining is a constructive activity requiring students to actively engage in their learning process. Active participation is better than passive participation for learning" (p. 92). The same could be said for every technique described in this book: all of them represent different avenues toward active engagement, but none of them should constitute your sole route to that active engagement. Think about self-explanation as the strategy that can prove especially helpful to your students as they are in the early and middle stages of mastering cognitive skills, from solving problems to writing papers, and as a possible spur to better self-understanding for any type of learner. Even small opportunities for students to self-explain, when they are embarked on their learning journey, can help steer them away from misunderstandings and back into the middle of the road.

Part III

Inspiration

T he final three chapters of this book stem from an acknowledgment of the fact that both learners and teachers are more than collections of neural networks, or receptacles of information, or practitioners of cognitive skills. They are fully realized human beings with emotions, attitudes, and other attributes that intersect with both teaching and learning. They need inspiration as much as, if not more than, they need knowledge and skills. Unfortunately, we tend to think first and foremost about how things like emotions and attitudes can *interfere* with learning. After all, we can all either envision or remember how powerful emotions might reduce learning in college courses. I full well remember falling in love with my then-future wife during my junior year in college and finding it very difficult to concentrate on anything but that burgeoning emotion and all of its attendant distractions. Hours that had previously been spent thinking deep thoughts (ahem) about my major courses in philosophy or literature became hours devoted to moony dreaming about the lovely face of my future spouse. And as happens with many college students, I experienced the death of grandparents during my college years. The weeks following those events represented another difficult moment for me to concentrate fully on my studies. On a more regular basis, college students in your courses might be distracted from learning by emotions that result from wrangling with their roommates, from constant appraisal and reappraisal of their social statuses, from their relationships with family and significant others, from failures and triumphs on the sports teams they support or play on, or from major world events or developments in the political causes they support.

Emotions have the power to enhance learning as much as they do to detract from it. George Orwell wrote, "The energy that actually shapes the world springs from emotions" (Orwell 1968, p. 141). That energy has powerful positive potential. Emotions such as awe and wonder can play an important role in orienting us toward learning tasks, and even negative emotions such as confusion or frustration can drive us in positive directions if we suspect that new learning will help resolve or eliminate those negative emotional states. One of my favorite formulations of what drives learning comes from Ken Bain's book *What the Best College Teachers Do* (Bain 2004). He drew on the work of Piaget and other learning theorists to argue that students bring mental models of the world into our classes, and much of our job as instructors consists of destroying any false models they might have, enhancing the partially correct ones, and providing accurate new ones. For us to do this, though, two conditions have to apply: we have to help the students recognize that their current mental models of the world are not adequate; and the students have to *care* that their mental models are not adequate (Bain 2004, pp. 26–32). If they don't care about the gap they perceive between their current models and the ones we can help them construct, they won't engage in the hard work of learning, which will enable them to build better models. Bain's formulation of the challenge that we face as teachers gives proper acknowledgment to the powerful role that emotions play in higher education: caring matters. If caring matters so much to our students and helps determine whether they really engage with our courses, shouldn't it also matter to us?

The same is true of attitudes. As we shall see from Carol Dweck's research (Dweck, 2008), how students think about intelligence and learning significantly impacts their willingness to tackle difficult cognitive tasks, their persistence through such tasks, their enjoyment of them, and even their performance of them. Students who carry damaging attitudes toward their own cognitive capacities face a serious handicap in their ability to learn. It probably will not surprise you that a student who doubts his cognitive capacities may give up in the face of difficult challenges, but it might surprise you to know that such doubts, when they are heightened by the practices or words of the teacher, *can actually diminish performance*. The large body of research first established by Dweck and now supported by other researchers demonstrates clearly that what students believe about their intelligence and their ability to change it impacts almost every aspect of the cognitive work that they must complete in our courses. Hence, we owe it to our students to think carefully about how our teaching and feedback practices might help shape student attitudes toward learning and intelligence in ways that will enhance their learning—or, at the very least, will not detract from it.

The small teaching techniques in the next two chapters and the theories that underlie them are as essential to producing deep learning as any of the techniques we have covered thus far. After all, asking students to predict and retrieve or self-explain won't get them very far in their learning if they truly don't care about the course material or if they believe that they are incapable of learning from it. My fellow writing teachers will have heard from at least one student over the course of their careers (and probably they will have heard it from many students, as I have) a statement along the lines of, "I'm not very good at writing." Of course you're not, I want to say to them: that's why you're here! Let's dig in and help you get better! But when students have deeply absorbed the belief that they are not good at writing, that belief can interfere with any efforts I might make to help them improve, however carefully designed they might be. Math teachers will know this phenomenon equally well, having heard from many of their students some variation of, "I'm no good at math." The problem arises because students who believe they are no good at *doing* math (or writing, of any other skill required by your courses) often also believe they are no good at *learning* math. That latter belief will sound a death knell for that student's learning in your course, no matter how smartly you are relying on cognitive principles in your course design and classroom practices.

The final chapter of this book arises from the conviction that teachers, over the course of a long career, also need inspiration. Just as we want students to adopt a positive and flexible attitude toward their learning, so must we. You should expect that over a 20- or 30- or 40-year teaching career you will have moments when you feel stuck in a pedagogical rut. You will undoubtedly have opportunities to step back and recharge your teaching batteries occasionally, whether that comes in the form of a sabbatical or even just 2 or 3 weeks between fall and spring semester. During those times, and throughout the various stages of your career, you might want to think about pushing into new territories as a teacher. As higher education continues to evolve in the face of rising cost pressures and technological innovation, I see some promising pathways for instructors to pursue when they are ready to experiment with larger pedagogical innovations than the ones we have been considering here. Therefore, the final chapter considers some approaches that fall under the umbrella of what I might call big teaching: large-scale, design-oriented approaches to higher education pedagogy that impact every aspect of a course from the objectives to the daily teaching practices. You might not be ready for such an approach right now—but you might be, or you might be at some future date. This chapter suggests some pathways to pedagogical revolution that are well grounded in what we know about how people learn and that should eventually repay the time and effort it will take you to implement them.

You might wonder, given the crucial role that motivation and attitudes can play in learning, why I have saved these for the final part of the book rather than opening with them. I did so because I wanted you to see first how small teaching changes can make a big difference to student learning, and one can see that principle displayed most clearly with concrete activities like retrieval or prediction or self-explaining. Thinking about inspiration, and about student emotions and attitudes, might seem like we are pushing into large and amorphous realms of the teaching and learning enterprise. However, we have excellent evidence, as we shall see in Dweck's work, for example, that small changes can make a major difference in these areas as well. We will therefore tackle motivation and attitude just as we have approached our previous theories, principles, and models—by thinking small.

Chapter 7

Motivating

INTRODUCTION

The oldest three of my five children all undertook music lessons of some form or another when they were in the younger grades of elementary school. My oldest daughter began with piano lessons, got bored, and switched to guitar; she got bored with that as well and then stopped altogether. The second oldest also took piano lessons, got bored, and stopped. Number three took a year of piano lessons, got bored, switched to violin lessons, got bored with those, and then stopped. Overall, our third daughter lasted the longest in her musical pursuits by a good 2 years, which was still not long enough to sustain her through middle school. After three iterations of this same experience, my wife and I decided to give the twins a pass and have not subjected them to this same frustrating (and expensive) cycle. In the case of our three eldest children, however, I can see a clear surface explanation for the recurrence of this cycle. All three expressed an initial interest in taking music lessons; it was not our idea. We have a piano in our living room, which I play occasionally, so they heard music around our house and must have been curious. That curiosity sustained them for the first weeks and months of their lessons, and they seemed to enjoy themselves in those early stages of their brief musical careers. They enjoyed going to lessons and, at first, practiced willingly. But, as anyone who has ever attempted to master a musical instrument knows, eventually you have to buckle down and engage in lots of practice (ideally mindful and creative practice, like the type described by Langer (1997) in her piano-playing experiment, but practice nonetheless). On the piano, this includes playing scales, which are like finger exercises that help you strengthen your muscles, master the positions of the notes on the keyboard, and learn the different key signatures of Western music. The further my children pushed into these types of practice exercises, the more their interest in their musical instruments waned. Initial interest and curiosity gave way to grudging and irregular bouts of practice and then finally to complete abandonment of the instrument—with one exception.

All three girls started lessons with the same piano teacher, who focused on teaching them classical music. When my third daughter took up violin, though, she found herself with a teacher who played folk and Irish music and who loved to teach her students those kinds of song. As it happens, I also love folk and Irish music, so my own occasional music playing—on the piano, accordion, and tin whistle—usually falls into those genres. As my daughter moved further along in her violin lessons and became capable of playing some songs that I knew, I would sometimes sit with her and we would play songs together. This was really the only time that she ever would practice without complaining—when I played with her. As we were discussing what she would play for her end-of-year recital, I proposed that we play a song together, with me accompanying her on the piano. She liked this idea, so for months and weeks in advance of the show we practiced together on her recital song. We enjoyed this process so much that when a friend asked me if I would play some music at a local church service he was organizing, I asked my daughter if she wanted to join me. She did, and thus ensued another round of enthusiastic practice. After that service, though, a series of obligations in my own life meant that I had to take a hiatus from doing much playing or practicing. Shortly after we stopped playing together, she decided that she didn't want to play violin anymore.

If you browse the research literature on motivation and learning, you will find frequent reference to a contrast between two overarching types of motivation: *intrinsic* or *internal motivation* versus *extrinsic* or *instrumental* motivation. Extrinsic motivators include the rewards that the learner expects to gain from successful learning, such as prizes or accolades or praise or even grades; intrinsic motivators are the ones that drive learners for their own internal reasons, such as love of the material or a recognition of its utility in their lives or of its ultimate value on some broader scale (e.g., their personal or spiritual development). According to this theory, the best and deepest learning takes place when it is driven by intrinsic motivators—when, in other words (and put simply), the learner cares about the learning itself or the matter to be learned rather than about some reward she will receive at the end of the learning period. Of course, this binary opposition between internal and external types of motivation hardly exhausts the field of motivation studies, which constitutes an entire subdiscipline crossing the borders of psychology and education. To give just one other example, Susan Ambrose and her colleagues argued in *How Learning Works* that another approach to motivation involves breaking it down into two elements: *subjective value* and *expectancies* (2010, p. 69). The extent to which the learning or the subject matter seems important to the individual learner represents its subjective value; the extent to which the learner feels as if her work and practice will lead to a positive outcome represents the learner's expectancies. Both of these elements must be present for motivation to be high.

Helping light the fires of intrinsic motivation in our students, or foster high subjective values, might seem like an unbeatable candidate for the Least Likely Subject for Small Teaching award. It sounds pretty idealistic to expect that 10-minute segments of class can suddenly infuse an 18-year-old with no interest in literature with a deep and abiding love of the British novel. Attempting to think about motivation in those terms, in my experience working with college and university instructors, can feel overwhelming. So in true small teaching fashion, we are going to step away from viewing motivation in terms of this ambitious goal and instead lock in on a very simple lever that psychologists have established as a powerful potential pump for human motivation: emotions. When my daughters all rubbed against the tough work of learning a musical instrument, their initial motivation—which may have been an intrinsic one, simply based on their curiosity about music—faltered and died away. Most of our students will experience such faltering in the motivation they bring to their courses, just as we experience such faltering in our own learning. Remember what you felt when you were on page 147 of your dissertation and couldn't stand the thought of writing another sentence? Your students feel the same way on Tuesday morning at 8:30 a.m. when they are facing another challenging problem set. What separated the musical experience of my third daughter from that of my older two was my participation in the process; what marked that participation as distinct was the presence of emotions in driving her learning. When I joined her on the piano, music practice became a shared social activity: we spoke and laughed together, we were physically close to one another, we worked cooperatively to join our melodies together. For her, as a 10-year-old, the process also undoubtedly became bundled into a younger child's natural desire to please and spend time with her parent.

Together we faced the frightening prospect of the recital and the church service and the triumphant feeling of conquering it. These kinds of emotions, both shared and individual, have strong motivational power.

Approaching motivation from the realm of emotions does not conflict in any way with thinking about motivation as intrinsic or extrinsic or reduce the scope of what we are attempting. Consider emotions as a motivating force that have the power to drive both intrinsically and extrinsically motivated learners under the right circumstances. Leveraging the power of positive emotions like purposefulness or wonder might help whip up the small flames of intrinsic motivation in students or provide timely boosts to extrinsically motivated students. After all, even learners with deep intrinsic motivation will need a push now and then to get them through the daily challenges of new learning. Students who are driven by extrinsic motivation, perhaps because their interests lie in other subjects, can still find themselves swept up by their emotions into a powerful learning experience in your course. Emotions, as we shall see, also represent the best route for practitioners of small teaching to pursue in seeking to motivate their students. We can leverage emotions into courses and classrooms in a host of small ways; in doing so, we are working with our shared neurological heritage to give them the motivation they might need to push through the next challenge to their learning. In this chapter, then, we shift the question from the usual one that teachers ask about student motivation—how can I foster internal or intrinsic motivation in my students?—to one that acknowledges the reality and power of emotions in the classroom: How can I elicit and work with the emotions already present in the room to give students frequent motivational boosts throughout the semester?

IN THEORY

Sarah Cavanagh is director of the Laboratory for Cognitive and Affective Science at Assumption College and author of *The Spark of Learning: Energizing the College Classroom with the Science of Emotion*, a powerful new analysis of how emotions impact learning in and outside our classrooms, especially in higher education. Cavanagh surveyed a large body of research that demonstrates the incredibly important role emotions play in almost every aspect of our lives, including in the teaching and learning process. "Emotions are at your side," she concludes,

> Guiding your hand in every decision you make, from which three plums to select from a basket of fruit to whether to leave your spouse. It is not hard, then, to suppose that emotions are similarly guiding our students in every stage of their learning, from selecting which courses to take in a given semester to how willing they are to participate in the discussion you're trying to drum up on the Tuesday before Thanksgiving. (Cavanagh 2016, p. 15)

You know this already, whether you are drawing on your experience as a learner or a teacher. You might know it from an experience like the one I described in the introduction to this part of the book, in which powerful emotions like love or grief interfered with your ability, as a student, to concentrate on a learning task or a course or even an entire semester's worth of courses. And you likely know it in more positive ways as well, such as when you were toiling away in the laboratory or reading in the library and had a sudden realization and became flush with the excitement and curiosity and happiness that sparked your dissertation or an article or book project or even an idea for a new course. Or you might know it in a more mixed way, when you felt stymied or frustrated or confused by something that drove you to resolve those emotions by learning something new.

Three key elements of the research on emotions and learning seem to me ripe for exploitation by college and university faculty, so we'll focus on those—although they don't by any means tell the whole story of the connections between emotions and learning. First, and most generally, emotions can help us *capture the attention of our students*. "Activating [student] emotions," Cavanagh wrote, "results in a number of cascading effects in the body and brain, all of which are designed to maximize cognitive and physical performance and make memories stronger" (p. 14). According to Cavanagh, this connection between our emotions and attention stems from the very reasons we have emotions in the first place. Emotions originally helped draw our attention to experiences that we might want to remember for survival purposes:

> Emotions were selected for because they both influence motivation—driving us toward things that are good for survival and reproduction (high-calorie foods, attractive sex partners) and away from things that threaten our health or well-being (venomous spiders, rotten food)—and because they influence learning, tagging certain experiences and skills as important and thus critical to both attend to and remember. (p. 14)

As our brains were evolving, emotions helped us recognize more carefully what was important to learn and remember from the range of experiences we encountered every day. Terror inspired by a predator helped us better remember to avoid that particular path through the woods; the pleasure experienced while eating that nutritious fruit helped us better remember what that tree looked like and where we might find it again tomorrow. The environment in which we live has changed, but we all continue to face socially, emotionally, and physically threatening challenges and driving pleasures. Our emotional brains continue to operate in these circumstances as they always have: when we feel strong emotions, our attention and cognitive capacities are heightened.

We don't want to whip up emotions in the classroom randomly, though; some emotions seem particularly helpful for deepening learning. A second line of research in this area, then, suggests that we focus on infusing learning with *a sense of purpose, and especially self-transcendent purpose*. In *How We Learn*, Benedict Carey noted first that purposefulness tunes the attention of learners toward things that matter: "Having a goal foremost in mind tunes our perceptions to fulfilling it. And that tuning determines, to some extent, where we look and what we notice" (p. 140). A sense of purpose drives our attention *toward* certain things and drives it *away from* other things, just as emotions like fear and pleasure do. So imagine that you are driving to meet a friend at an unfamiliar location in an unfamiliar town. You are looking for a red building on Elm Street. Everything you see and pay attention to runs through those two filters: Is it Elm Street? Is it a red building? After you have arrived at the red building on Elm Street, with your attention having been so focused on the route, you would be likely to recount to your friend exactly how you got there but very unlikely to describe the general layout of the city, the number of black buildings you passed, or the woman in the blue dress who was waiting to cross the street as you drove by. Your sense of purpose tuned your focus to what mattered to you and helped you achieve your specific goal. If we can help create that sense of purpose in our students and can ensure that their purpose aligns with what we want them to learn, we are likely to heighten their attention and cognitive capacities in our courses and to turn their minds in productive directions.

A particularly fascinating new line of research in this area can refine our small teaching work ever further, since it suggests that not all senses of purpose are equal—and that the most powerful forms of purposefulness arise when students see the ability of their learning to make the world a better place. In 2014 a handful of researchers published a long study, wonderfully titled "Boring but Important," which explored what types of purposefulness most inspired learners to persist in learning repetitive or challenging yet essential tasks for future learning or academic success (Yeager, Henderson, Paunesku, Walton, D'Mello, Spitzer, and Duckworth 2014). The surprising result of this research was that self-transcendent purpose produced the strongest driver for students to persist through challenging academic tasks. Self-transcendent motivation contrasts with self-oriented motivation, which describes a desire to have a great career or enhance one's knowl-edge or abilities. Self-transcendent motivation describes a desire to help other people, to change the world in some positive way, to make a difference. The superior power of self-transcendent motivation appeared first in surveys of low-income high school seniors who planned to attend college the next fall. (The ones who had the highest levels of self-transcendent purpose were most likely to actually enroll.) However, it also appeared in experiments in which college students who were faced with the prospect of solving or studying difficult review questions before a final exam were reminded beforehand about the self-transcendent power of their learning:

> Results showed that a self-transcendent purpose for learn-ing increased the tendency to attempt to learn deeply from tedious academic tasks ... Students spent twice as long on their review questions when they had just written about

how truly understanding the subject area could allow them to contribute to the world beyond the self, compared to controls. (p. 571)

As long as we are thinking about how to infuse our student learning with purpose, we may be getting the largest possible bang for our buck if we can help them recognize the power of their learning to make a difference to the world: in doing so we are both helping direct their attention and giving them the motivation to persist through learning challenges.

Third and finally, emotions are *social*—which helps explain one aspect of the experience I had with my daughter. When I became interested in learning her recital song, she became interested in learning it, too. Borrowing a phrase from Marjorie Keller, this is why Cavanagh calls emotions a *contagious fire*: they can be catching. Again, let personal experience be your best example here. How often, when you are home alone watching a television sitcom or comedy film, do you find yourself laughing out loud? Far less frequently, I would wager, than you find yourself laughing out loud when you are watching a comedy with a group of friends or watching a film in a theater. Humans are social animals, and we feed off each other's emotions. This is as true in the classroom as it is in the movie theater. The most concrete way this contagion has been analyzed in the classroom relates to the enthusiasm of the teacher and the effect that strong enthusiasm can have on student learning. For example, Cavanagh pointed to a study in which researchers measured markers of enthusiasm among teachers of secondary students in a Swiss school and found a startling correlation between those markers and the experiences of the students in the classroom: "The enthusiasm of the educators statistically predicted their students' ratings of enjoyment and perceived value in the subject matter" (Cavanagh 2016, p. 64). This latter finding represents the one we should pay special attention to. Remember that Ambrose et al. (2010) identified subjective value as one of the key drivers of motivation in education, and we can see here that teacher enthusiasm positively impacted precisely this quality, here described as perceived value in the subject matter. The emotions that we demonstrate to students, especially our positive emotions connected to the subject matter we are teaching, can create a strong positive boost to student motivation.

The social connection between you and your students tells only part of the story, though. Of course your students far outnumber you in the room, and it seems equally to be the case that students' emotions have a powerful potential to boost each other's motivation for learning. Dan Chambliss and Christopher Takacs demonstrated in their book *How College Works* (2014) the immense power that personal connections and relationships have on the total college experience for students, including the learning that takes place in the classroom. "What really matters in college," they argue, "is who meets whom, and when" (p. 16). These conclusions stem from a long-term study they conducted on students and alumni at their institution, based on a variety of measures, including interviews, surveys, and analyses of student work. One of the key areas in which they saw social relationships and community as playing an essential role was motivation: "Motivation is crucial … and emotional connections to others and to a community provide the strongest motivation" (p. 106). Students relay their levels of motivation through the amount of effort they put into their studying and assignments, through the ways they talk about their courses, through their classroom behaviors such as speaking (or not speaking) in class or participating in group work. As they do so, they are conveying emotional signals—this subject matters to me; I am enjoying this discussion; this professor is boring me—that their fellow students will catch and respond to. I've learned from my own experience as a teacher that a few engaged and highly motivated students can energize an entire class; a few students openly displaying signs of boredom or frustration can likewise derail one. As Jay Howard has written in *Discussion in the College Classroom*, "the most important learning and the most effective learning happens through a social process" (Howard 2015, p. 110). Both faculty and students play a crucial role in creating and determining the shape of that social process.

At this point you might be wondering whether I am going to recommend group hand holding or inspirational speeches to create the best emotional climate in your classroom for learning. Don't worry—I'm not a group hand holding kind of person, and I won't recommend here (or anywhere in this book) strategies that I wouldn't be willing to try myself or that I haven't tried already. The models that follow, in fact, might not strike you as connected to emotion and motivation in obvious ways; I hope they will strike you as sensible teaching practices that might fit into your classroom even if you want to avoid thinking about the emotions of your students. Just know that these six models should provide the kind of positive, activating emotional boost your students need to push through the daily and weekly challenges of your courses—and they just may inspire some of them into the kind of deep and lifelong engagement that all teachers dream about for their students.

MODELS

The following models argue both for emotions that you can activate in your students, such as curiosity and purpose, and ones that you can activate in yourself, such as enthusiasm and compassion. All of them should help provide a motivational push toward better learning.

Get to Class Early, Part 1

Peter Newbury is an astronomer who now serves as associate director of the Center for Engaged Teaching at the University of California at San Diego. In a wonderful little blog post on the center's website titled "You Don't Have to Wait for the Clock to Strike to Start Teaching," he described a teaching activity that offers an ideal example of how to model emotions such as curiosity and wonder to capture the attention of his students at the start of class. Drawing inspiration from the "Astronomy Picture of the Day," a NASA website that posts a new and fascinating image from the cosmos every day, he suggests that instructors begin classes—even before class officially begins—by posting an image on the screen at the front of the room and asking two questions about it: What do you notice? What do you wonder? Let the image direct the informal conversations or reflections of the students prior to the start of class, and then use it to guide a brief discussion during the opening minutes of class. Newbury suggested that this strategy can help accomplish multiple objectives, many of which have been covered in other chapters in this book. For example, such an activity can activate students' prior knowledge, thereby helping them form connections with what they already know; it also offers wonderful opportunities for learning activities such as prediction and retrieval. Obviously you could substitute anything for the NASA picture of the day: a great sentence in a writing class; a newspaper headline in a political science class; an audio clip for a music class; a physical object in an archeology class.

What this small teaching technique really strikes me as accomplishing is a message from the instructor that hits on several of the motivational emotions we have considered already: I find this stuff fascinating, and I think you will too. Let's wonder together about it. I can't think of a better way to begin (or pre-begin) a learning experience with your students.

Get to Class Early, Part 2

I had the opportunity to attend an event recently on my campus in which we discussed how individual relationships with students can impact their learning. A faculty member offered the following fascinating contribution to this discussion. She was an introvert, she said, but she had decided that she wanted to make a more deliberate effort to connect with the students in her classroom. So in the previous semester she had shown up to every class session 5–10 minutes early and—even though she found it a struggle—spent a few of those minutes approaching individuals in the class and engaging in casual conversation. She did so in a carefully planned way, ensuring that she approached every student at least once over the course of the semester: "Even that stony-faced kid sitting in the back row—I made sure I spoke to him too." When her student evaluations came in after the semester had ended, she was quite surprised to find that multiple students noted this simple practice of hers as something that contributed to the overall positive atmosphere in the classroom. What struck her about this particular experience that differed from previous semesters was that in the past she might have engaged in occasional patter with the students in the front row; this semester she made the effort to speak to each student individually at least once.

To help understand why this small gesture might matter so much to students and how it connects to their emotions, consider one of the more fascinating findings from Chambliss and Takacs's study reported in *How College Works* (2014). In collaboration with others at their institution, the authors analyzed a massive survey of student writing at their college, trying to determine whether student writing improved over the course of a student's 4 years. One surprising result of this analysis was that many students demonstrated very fast gains in writing in their first year of college—sometimes within weeks or months of arriving at the college. This happens less because of any specific instruction, they concluded, than it does for the very simple reason that instructors at the college they studied make a strong commitment to responding to student papers, both in their comments and in individual student conferences. When the students see that instructors are actually reading and critiquing their work, they become motivated to work a little harder at their writing—and that harder work pays off in some immediate gains in their writing abilities. As Chambliss and Takacs explained, "What mattered from professors was the sheer fact of paying attention: she took the time; he helped me. Attention says to the student, 'Writing matters'; but more, it says, '*Your* writing matters'" (p. 112, italics in original). This suggests that the sheer fact of paying attention to student work spurs a motivational boost. In the same way, my colleague's experience suggests that paying attention to students in class made a noticeable difference in creating a positive atmosphere in her classroom and even—as she explained to us later—increased the number of students who participated in classroom discussions.

Technology can help both face-to-face and online teachers create these motivational connections with their students, as Jose Bowen notes in *Teaching Naked* (Bowen 2012). He urges faculty to use electronic communications and social media to "create communities" and "connect with students" (p. 30). If you have students create brief videos to introduce themselves to the class, make a comment on each of those videos. If they write discussion posts or blogs that do this, make sure you comment on each one, something more than "Welcome to the class!" If you have a class Twitter feed, reply to and favorite student tweets. These communication media can help us recognize students as individuals as effectively as a friendly preclass chat.

But if you have a face-to-face component to your course, see if you can find ways to use the periphery of the class period—those minutes before class starts, or after class starts, or outside of the strict content of your online courses—to pay attention to the learners in your course. Chambliss and Takacs's research suggests that this very simple act can boost the learning motivation of your students.

Tell Great Stories

Once class has started, the simplest way to tap the emotions of your students is to use the method that every great orator, comedian, emcee, and preacher knows: begin with a story. Human beings are storytelling and story-loving animals. As cognitive psychologist Daniel Willingham put it, "The human mind seems exquisitely tuned to understand and remember stories—so much so that psychologists sometimes refer to stories as 'psychologically privileged,' meaning that they are treated differently in memory than other types of material" (Willingham 2009, pp. 66–67). Willingham pointed to the results of experiments demonstrating that people seem to find stories as having a special power to capture and maintain interest: "Reading researchers have conducted experiments in which people read lots of different types of materials and rate each for how interesting it is. Stories are consistently rated as more interesting than other formats (for example, expository prose) even if the same information is presented" (p. 68). Willingham and other researchers posit a number of different possible reasons for this, but one clear reason to me seems to be that the best stories invoke emotions. Stories have the power to induce laughter, sorrow, puzzlement, and anger. Indeed, I would be hard-pressed to think of a great story that did not produce emotions of some kind. We learned from Sarah Cavanagh that when emotions are present, our cognitive capacities can heighten; so if we can open class by capturing the attention of our students and activating their emotions with a story, we are priming them to learn whatever comes next.

You probably have plenty of stories you tell during your lectures or discussions. Perhaps you tell the stories of how certain key discoveries were made in your discipline; perhaps you tell stories about the famous people who have been major thinkers in your field; perhaps you tell stories about experiences you have had that connect to your course topics; perhaps you tell stories about things that you encounter in your daily reading, or in the news, or in movies or television shows you love. All these stories might appear in random points throughout your course, or perhaps you use them to illustrate certain key ideas when they crop up throughout the class period. The small teaching recommendation here is simply to be more deliberate about your use of stories. Take your best story and open with it. Then make sure that you are regularly renewing and recapturing the attention of your students with a story every now and then. Ideally, you should use an opening story that will help pique the interest of your students in the material to come in that class period, in addition to activating an emotion or two. For example, on the day that I introduce Romantic literature in my British literature survey course, I have historically given a lecture about the economic disparities that existed during that time and that drove many writers to focus their writing on the poor and outcast members of society. This lecture went about as well as most of my lectures go—meh—until I discovered in my own reading a heart-wrenching newspaper story from that time period of a child chimney sweep who was beaten to death by his master. My lecture on the economics of the Romantic period now opens with two stories: the tale of this poor chimney sweep and the tale of the coronation party of the prince regent, which was one of the most lavish affairs ever held in England at that time. These two stories, first individually and then taken together, help draw the students in and set them up for the statistics on wealth and income inequality that will follow. At the end of the semester, on the final essay exam for the course, I find that students still will remember the story of that chimney sweep and the spendthrift prince regent and will use them in their answers on the literature of the Romantic period.

Another way of thinking about the use of stories in your class would be to follow a suggestion made by Willingham and frame a class as a story: "Organizing a lesson plan like a story is an effective way to help students comprehend and remember" (p. 67). For example, you might open class with the first half of a story, one that should leave your students puzzled and wondering what comes next. Then launch into the class, explaining that they will now need some information or ideas or theories to better understand how to resolve that puzzle. At the close of class, finish the story. Another way to think about this would be to open the class with a question, one that the class period will help the students answer. As Willingham wrote, "The material I want students to learn is actually the answer to a question. *On its own the answer is almost never interesting.* But if you know the question, the answer may be quite interesting" (p. 75; italics in original). In sum, consider how you can use the opening and closing minutes of class to set students up with a fascinating question or story opener that gets resolved by the end of the class period. The bulk of what you do within the class might change very little in this model; what changes is the frame, which you tweak in classic small teaching fashion.

Invoke Purpose—Especially Self-Transcendent Purpose

Over the course of a semester, students—perhaps like instructors—are going to occasionally lose sight of the bigger picture. When they are dug in and working on a specific and thorny problem-solving exercise during the seventh week of the term, they may forget that you are ultimately teaching them skills that will help them pass the CPA exam or will enable them to become successful entrepreneurs, or will provide them with the skills they need to end world hunger. Students need regular invocations of the larger purpose of individual exercises, class periods, and course units. The authors of a large-scale study of motivation among West Point cadets both during college and throughout their army careers argued that regular invocations of purpose are essential to creating a climate that fosters and rewards deep, intrinsic motivation. Although they used language appropriate to business organizations, the findings translate easily into education:

> If organizations do little or nothing to emphasize their purposes, aside—for example—from earning profits, internal motives may wither while instrumental motives become ascendant. Small but regular reminders of organizational purpose can keep internal motives dominant … a range of meaningful consequences should be highlighted (e.g., impact on others, mastery). (Wrzesniewski, 10995)

As we saw from the "Boring but Important" study (Yeager, Henderson, Paunesku, Walton, D'Mellow, Spitzer, and Duckworth 2014), the meaningful consequences that may prove most effective for your students are those that emphasize the power of your discipline to help their fellow human beings or to make a positive impact on the world in some way. You will have to begin the process of motivating students in this way by reminding yourself of the reasons that your discipline does matter—something we can lose sight of after years of teaching or in the long slog of the semester. In the middle of a composition course, I'm not always thinking about the fact that powerful pieces of writing or oratory have turned the tide against slavery, have created new nations, or have inspired people to drop everything and dedicate their lives to the poor. However, I know these things are true, and they have inspired me. They can do the same for my students.

When the authors of the West Point study spoke of small but regular reminders that invoke purpose, they were speaking the language of small teaching. Such reminders about the larger purpose of your course can and should appear in any of the following ways:

- *On your syllabus.* Tune the language of your course description to the promises that your course makes to them rather than to the subject material that you will be covering. What skills will students develop that will enable them to make a difference in the world? What purpose will the learning they have done serve in their lives, their futures, their careers? Invoke this language from the first day of the course.
- *On individual assignments.* Draw from that syllabus language in every assignment. Use words and phrases that tie each assignment at least one step up toward your course promises: "This paper assignment is designed to help you develop your skills in crafting a thesis and using evidence to support an argument ... These presentations should prepare you to make effective sales pitches to organizations or groups ... "
- *On the board, real or virtual.* The simplest way to connect individual class periods to the course purpose is to keep that connection in front of their face during class, real or virtual. Have a simple but overarching course or unit outline that you can write on the board each class period, and then note exactly where this class falls within that larger picture. This could be done on the actual board or on your course website's individual pages.
- *In the opening and closing minutes of class.* Use those coveted time periods to remind students where they have been, where you are now, where you are going, and—most important—*why*.

As long as you have made your initial case about the purpose of your course effectively, on your syllabus and in the opening weeks of the semester, you should need only small reminders to help students reconnect to that purpose throughout the term.

Share Your Enthusiasm

If you want students to care about the material, you not only have to care about it yourself—which I will take for granted that you do—but also have to *demonstrate to them* that you care about it. You can find lots and lots of research in the educational literature on the role that teacher enthusiasm plays in inspiring students to learn, and you can find plenty of grumpy responses from instructors who claim that they should not have to dance around and sing the praises of the material to inspire student learning. At one point in my career, I remember reading a bunch of the literature on this subject and having this same grumpy reaction, which stemmed from my more introverted leanings. At that time I was teaching an upper-level seminar on British literature, and the students were participating very well in our class discussions. They didn't need my enthusiasm or inspiration anymore, I reasoned. So I prepared very thoroughly for the next class but decided that I was not going to do what I normally did at that time—namely, sweeping into the classroom with lots of energy and attempting to spark their discussions with my own enthusiasm for the book we were reading. I came into class that day and sat down in the midst of the students at the long table in our seminar room, without any preliminary inspirational opening, and spoke very quietly about the book we were reading for a few minutes. Then I attempted to start a conversation. In 15 years of teaching, that class was the worst class I have ever experienced. Even though I have probably taught thousands of individual class sessions, I still remember vividly not only the horrible feeling of being in that lifeless classroom but also the profound sense I felt afterward of being *so completely wrong*. I realized at that moment that no matter how great my students are or how well the class is going, I still have to inject some of the energy into the room. To put it in the terms of Sarah Cavanagh's book, for a contagious fire to alight in my classroom, I have to start the process by striking the match.

With that said, you still don't need to dance around and sing to demonstrate to your students that you care about this material, that it matters to some larger context (their lives, their community, the world), and that you want it to matter to them. You can do this quietly, with occasional asides in class about the moments in your own learning that really sparked your interest or led you toward some exciting new discovery. Or you can do it by noting when the course arrives at the material that you find most interesting or important: Of all the books we are reading this semester, this one's my absolute favorite—I've read it 20 times and still find new insights in it; this particular problem never fails to fascinate me; I have been waiting all semester to get to this point because now we are facing the most intriguing challenge that most of you will confront in your careers. The small teaching recommendation here simply involves allowing the enthusiasm that you felt when you were first studying your discipline—or that you show to your peers and colleagues when you are talking about your favorite features of your discipline—show in your classroom as well. The personality that appears when I am talking to a colleague in the hallway about the most recent book from my favorite novelist should find its way into my classroom. That can happen in lots of small ways; it takes only a deliberate decision to open that side of yourself to your students in as many class periods as possible. You'll have your dull and uninspiring days, as we all do. But take a few minutes before you head over to class each day to just pause and reconnect with whatever you find most fascinating about that day's material, and let it rise to the surface of your mind—allowing it to remain there throughout class.

Of course, if you're a dance-and-sing kind of person when it comes to enthusiasm, then just follow your instincts. Dance and sing.

Show Compassion

Remember what you were like at 18 or 19 or 20 years old. Then remember what it was like to have a powerful emotional experience at that age, especially a negative or distracting one. Your grandmother has died and you are devastated by the loss. Or you failed an exam in one of your major courses and you might lose your scholarship. Or your father lost his job and is no longer sure he can help you pay for your college costs, and you are wondering whether all of this time and energy you are spending in college is worth it. You manage to write a paper during this period, and turn it in to meet a deadline even though you know it's not your best work. And then you get the paper back a week later, while you are still caught up in the emotional stew of your experience, and the teacher's comments include a hectoring lecture about your recent lack of attentiveness in class and your failure to pay attention to detail in your Works Cited page. Maybe you were a better 20-year-old than me, but my reaction would have been something along the following lines: "Given everything I am going through right now, does any of this stuff you are asking me to do *really* matter?" And, truth be told, that seems like a reasonable question to me even now. So the best advice I can offer here, even in small teaching terms, would be this: whenever you are tempted to come down hard on a student for any reason whatsoever, take a couple of minutes to speculate on the possibility that something in the background of that student's life has triggered emotions that are interfering with their motivation or their learning. Just a few moments of reflection on that possibility should be enough to moderate your tone and ensure that you are offering a response that will not send that student deeper into a spiral of negative or distracting emotions, thus potentially preventing future learning from happening in your course.

PRINCIPLES

Use these three basic principles to guide both your motivational strategies and your own reading on this most important of topics for teachers at any level.

Acknowledge the Emotions in the Room They are there. You can't do anything about that. Rather than see that as a negative, instead look at the positive possibilities. You can tell stories, show film clips or images, make jokes, or do any number of things that will briefly activate the emotions of your students and prepare them to learn. You can leverage the power of emotions to heighten the cognitive capacities of your students at the opening, midway point, or closing of a course or a class period. Psychologist Michelle Miller, the author of *Minds Online*, encouraged instructors to ask themselves the following two questions: "What is the emotional heart of the material I am teaching? And how can I foreground this emotional center to my students?" (Miller 2014, p. 112).

Make It Social Use the contagious nature of emotions to your advantage. Give students the opportunity to learn together, to learn from one another, and to learn with you. If you are having a discussion, and it takes an interesting but potentially distracting turn, consider whether the value of letting the room heat up with some emotional conversation outweighs the goal of staying exactly on topic. If you are giving a lecture, don't hesitate to invite students into your monologue with jokes, stories, or questions. Give students who are working in groups the opportunity to tackle shared challenges that force them to rely on one another and cooperate like the social animals they are.

Show Enthusiasm First, care about your course material. If you are not excited by what you are teaching, and if you do not care deeply about it, don't expect your students to care about it either. But they won't know that you care deeply about it unless you are willing to show that to them, however that might seem best to you. Second, care about your students' learning. That means acknowledging that they are full human beings, not cognition machines, and the noncognitive parts of them sometimes will distract them from learning tasks. Let that awareness hover in your mind as you interact with students who are not performing as you think they should, and allow it to govern the tone—not necessarily the content—of your response to them.

SMALL TEACHING QUICK TIPS: MOTIVATING

Students bring into our courses a complex mix of backgrounds, interests, and motivations, and we can't turn every student into a passionate devotee of our discipline. We can, however, help create better learning in our courses with attention to some small, everyday motivational practices that have the power to boost both attention and learning.

- Get to class early every day and spend a few minutes getting to know your students, learning about their lives and their interests, and creating a positive social atmosphere in the room.
- Open individual class or learning sessions (and even readings) by eliciting student emotions: give them something to wonder about, tell them a story, present them with a shocking fact or statistic. Capture their attention and prepare their brains for learning.
- Consider how practitioners in your field, or the skills you are teaching them, help make a positive difference in the world;

remind them continually, from the opening of the course, about the possibility that their learning can do the same.

· Keep the overarching purpose of any class period or learning activity in view while students are working. Use the board or frequent oral reminders.

· Show enthusiasm for your discipline, for individual texts or problems or units, and for your hope that they will find them as fascinating as you do.

CONCLUSION

Before we conclude, I should acknowledge that some negative emotions have the power to create learning just as positive ones do. Miller actually suggested that "the less pleasant emotions tend to win out when it comes to memory ... negative emotions—fear, anger, and so forth—actually accentuate memory" (Miller 2014, p. 97). I always like to illustrate this point by recounting the story of the time when our dog shot out of the back door of our house and into the backyard to confront a trespassing animal he spied back there and was promptly sprayed in the face by a skunk. The next time he had the opportunity to approach the backyard, he did so with the full weight of that trauma in his memory and in an impossibly ginger manner, stepping one foot forward at a time, slowly and cautiously. To this day, more than 3 years later, he still approaches the backyard with trepidation, his senses obviously on high alert, as the memory of that foul encounter clearly lives on his learning brain.

We don't want to create traumatic experiences for students in our courses, even if they can help accentuate memory. While those emotions might imprint a learning experience deeply on our students' brains, they also might lead them to fear and avoid any future learning experience in that discipline or course or with that teacher. In certain limited cases we can stoke up negative emotions like outrage or sadness to help capture the attention of our students and drive them to action, but we have to do so cautiously. The use of such emotions should always lead to resolution in some form; if you stir up outrage over wealth inequality, the students should have the opportunity to talk about it, address it in their assignments, and process the experience. A safer route is to focus on the use of positive emotions to heighten the cognitive capacities of our students. We can inspire awe and wonder in them by leading them to the mysteries or problems or challenges of our disciplines; we can tap into their social selves by creating a dynamic, collaborative environment in our classrooms or in their group projects; we can invoke purpose by linking their classroom work to some brighter future or greater good for themselves or the world.

Whatever we do, we have to remember that the brains in our classrooms do more than think: they feel, and those feelings can play a valuable role in our efforts to motivate and inspire student learning.

Chapter 8

Growing

INTRODUCTION

In the late 1990s, Carol Dweck and Claudia Mueller, two psychologists then at Columbia University, conducted an experiment to see how the type of praise we give to children after they have completed a learning task influences their approach to future learning tasks (Mueller and Dweck 1998). Do certain types of praise have more positive effects than others? They noted in the introduction to the published essay on their experiment that many teachers and parents seem to believe that praising children for their natural talents or abilities will improve their learning and performance. "One can identify a lay theory of achievement motivation," they write, "in which praise for intelligence makes children feel smart and feeling smart, in turn, motivates learning" (p. 33). However, Dweck and Mueller had a different and contrary hypothesis, based in part on some previous research of their own. They believed that when children were praised for their natural talents and abilities, it could actually have detrimental effects on their future learning. Such praise could lead children to believe that intelligence is a stable and unchangeable trait, which might hinder children's willingness to work hard to improve themselves or take on challenging learning tasks. The opposite of this kind of *ability praise* would be *effort praise*: lauding children for the hard work they had put into a learning task and their attempts to overcome obstacles. This kind of praise, according to Dweck and Mueller's hypothesis, would perhaps not establish debilitating beliefs about the stability of intelligence and would instead encourage children to set ambitious learning goals and work hard to achieve them.

To test their hypotheses, Dweck and Mueller gave more than 100 fifth graders, from two very different population sets (one urban and multiracial, one Midwestern and mostly white), 4 minutes to solve 10 math problems. At the end of the 4 minutes, all the children were first praised for their achievement: "Wow, you did very well on these problems" (p. 36). Then some of the children were given additional praise of two different types (a control group received no additional praise). One group of children received some additional ability praise: "You must be smart at these problems" (p. 36). A second group was given effort praise: "You must have worked hard at these problems" (p. 36). After this second praise period, all the children were given 10 additional, much more difficult problems. No matter how well they did on these problems, all were told they performed "a lot worse" this time around. This was designed to give the children a setback in their learning and to test how they would respond to failure. In the final step of the experiment, the children were given a third set of 10 problems to solve, at the same level of difficulty as the first set. Dweck and Mueller used multiple measures, throughout and after the problem-solving sessions, to measure how the children thought about intelligence, learning, and their performance on the tasks.

The types of praise that the children received turned out to have wide-ranging effects on the children and their attitudes, motivation, and performance. For example, the children who had been praised for their natural abilities "enjoyed the tasks less than did the children praised for effort" (p. 37). More disturbingly, "children praised for intelligence were less likely to want to persist on the problems than children praised for effort" (p. 37). What helps explain findings like this is a deeper lesson that the children seemed to be learning about the nature of intelligence and about the connection between their intellectual *ability* and their *performance* on the problem sets.

> Children praised for intelligence appeared to learn that performance reflected their ability and thus attributed low performance to low ability. Children praised for hard work, on the other hand, did not show such a marked tendency to measure their intelligence from how well they did on the problems. (p. 37)

In other words, the ability-praised children came to believe that their performance on the problem sets reflected clearly on their natural intellectual abilities. Children praised for their efforts, by contrast, believed that their performance reflected the effort they had put into the problems. This distinction has clear and profound implications. If children tie their beliefs about intelligence to particular performances, it means that they will attribute poor performance—such as a low score on an exam—to low or deficient intelligence. In other words, rather than seeing a low exam score as the result of not enough studying, a bad day, or some other understandable reason, they will think, "I did not do a good job on this exam. I must be stupid." The children who had been praised for intelligence thought like this. The children who had been praised for their effort did not think this way. They attributed their poor performance to their lack of effort on the second set of problems and buckled down to work harder on the third set.

These types of results confirmed Dweck and Mueller's hypothesis: praise for effort, instead of praise for ability, will motivate children to work harder and persist in the face of challenges and will even increase their enjoyment of learning-oriented tasks. However, something really astonishing appeared when the researchers compared the scores of the two differently praised groups on the third set of problems, the ones the students received after their "poor" showing on the second set, which were of the same level of difficulty as the first set of problems they had completed. The type of praise the children received seemed to impact *even their performance* on this third set or problems: "Scores for children receiving intelligence feedback dropped an average of .92 ... Children in the effort condition, however, improved their prefailure scores by 1.21" (p. 38). Dweck and Mueller pointed out that these results are especially surprising because all three sets of 10 problems were similar in nature, differing only in level of difficulty: "These results are particularly striking because they demonstrate that the scores of children praised for intelligence decreased after failure even though their increased familiarity with the tasks should have bolstered, not weakened, their skills" (p. 38). In other words, everyone's scores should have been improving somewhat, since they were practicing multiple examples of the same problem type. That didn't happen, though, for the group praised for their intelligence; their scores dropped. It makes excellent sense to me that the praise we give to learners might impact their attitudes toward learning tasks or toward their enjoyment of those tasks. That it actually *decreased their performance* on the problems strikes me as both profound and potentially troubling for those of us who are charged with praising (or critiquing) learners for their performances on learning tasks.

IN THEORY

This experiment, and many more like it conducted by Dweck and other colleagues, led her eventually to formulate the theory of mind-set, which can help explain what was happening in the minds of those fifth graders and also will form the focus of this chapter. She provided the most full and rich description of this theory in her book *Mindset: The New Psychology of Success* (2008). People have either a *fixed* or *growth* mind-set when it comes to their attitudes and beliefs about learning and intelligence. Individuals with a fixed mind-set believe that their intelligence is a fixed, stable quantity; someone or something stamped an IQ on their forehead at birth, and they are limited to that IQ for the remainder of their lives. Individuals with a growth mind-set, in contrast, believe that intelligence is malleable and can improve with hard work and effort. Perhaps they recognize that they must work within certain limitations, but they see themselves as capable of growing and improving throughout their lives. Although Dweck's early research in this area focused on how mind-set influenced children in the types of learning tasks outlined in the introduction to this chapter, she came to believe that it influenced people in many aspects of their lives: "*The view you adapt for yourself* profoundly affects the way you lead your life. It can determine whether you become the person you want to be and whether you accomplish the things you value" (p. 6, italics in original). In support of this broadening of her theory, Dweck explored in the book how the debilitating effects of the fixed mind-set and the positive effects of the growth mind-set have influenced major figures in the world of sports and business as well as people's successes and failures in teaching, parenting, and relationships.

If you need an easy confirmation that mind-set plays a role in the lives of your students, walk down the hallway or across campus and step into the office of the first math professor you see. Ask her how many times she has heard students say some variation of this sentence: "I'm not very good at math." You will likely need a math professor to help keep track of the tally. You can probably also walk into the office of any English professor on your campus and pose the same question about this statement: "I'm not a very good writer." These are classic examples of fixed–mind-set statements, and they absolutely infect the classrooms of math and writing instructors on college campuses, not to mention other types of courses that rely heavily on mathematical skills or writing skills. Dweck's mind-set theory would suggest that a profound gulf exists between students who make statements like this and students who might recognize that they are not very good at math *right now* but believe that will change over the course of the semester. If you believe you are not good at math and that you have no hope of changing that, the implications of this belief spill out generously: first, you will avoid math whenever possible; second, if confronted with a context in which you must study or learn math, you will choose the least challenging possible route; third, you will find the whole process pointless and depressing, since each time you fail at a math problem it will simply confirm your negative self-assessment of your math abilities. It seems clear enough that we should want students in our courses with growth mind-sets and that we should seek to counter fixed mind-sets wherever we find them.

Before we consider the issue of how we might address our students' mind-sets, though, it's essential to pause and note that the growth mind-set better reflects what neuroscientists and cognitive psychologists tell us about our brains and our capacities for growth and learning: we *can* improve our intelligence through hard work and effort, and we can make ourselves smarter. We can get better at math, or writing, or whatever else we want to learn. The potential is not unlimited; it is more likely the case that we each have an intelligence range within which we fall, but that range can be very broad and our effort and attitude help determine whether we are growing within that range or remaining stuck in the same place. Dweck describes it like this: "Scientists are learning that people have more capacity for lifelong learning and brain development than they ever thought. Of course, each person has a unique genetic endowment. People may start with different temperament and different aptitudes, but it is clear that experience, training, and personal effort take them the rest of the way" (p. 5).

So it may not be the case that I can begin studying math this summer and end up with the Fields Medal by my next birthday. However, it may certainly be the case that I could start brushing up on my rusty old math skills this summer and make some real improvements in my capabilities by the time next summer rolls around. And I'm sure almost every math teacher who has been in the business for a while has a story to tell about students who believed they weren't very good at math and ultimately ended up succeeding in their courses in spite of themselves.

To understand how someone with such a fixed mind-set could blossom into a successful math student requires understanding a second essential point about mind-sets: *mind-sets can change*. In fact, as has been shown in multiple experiments by Dweck and her colleagues and a line of researchers who have taken up her work, mind-sets can change as the result of very simple and brief interventions. Knowing this will help you better understand what Dweck and Mueller were after in their experiment with those fifth-grade students. When they were praising students for their ability, they were attempting to nudge them toward a fixed mind-set. When they were praising children for their effort, they were attempting to nudge them toward a growth mind-set. We can assume that the children going into the experiment likely had been praised for their efforts or their abilities or some combination of both by well-meaning teachers throughout the first 5 years of their formal education. It seems equally likely that they would have heard effort- or ability-based praise from their parents for the previous 10 years as well. So they likely were carrying mind-sets, perhaps inchoate and unarticulated ones, into the experiment. Despite the fact that they already had certain mind-sets about learning and school, it took only a few words of carefully designed praise, either for ability or effort, to nudge them effectively into a fixed or growth mind-set. Ability praise encouraged the students to think that they were naturally smart, which discouraged additional effort; effort praise encouraged the students to think that working a little harder would make a difference in their performance on the math problems.

The power of mind-set and our ability to change it is not just for fifth graders, as multiple experiments and examples (including from higher education) from Dweck and other researchers demonstrate. (Note that in both of the next two studies, the researchers use the more technical terms for mind-set: *incremental theorists* for people with the growth mind-set and *entity theorists* for those with a fixed mind-set.) Consider, for example, a series of studies conducted by Laura Kray and Michael Haselhuhn on the mind-sets of students in an MBA course on negotiating (Kray and Haselhuhn, 2007). In one of their experiments, they measured students' mind-sets at the beginning of the course by asking them the extent to which they agreed with statements like, "Good negotiators are born that way" or "All people can change even their most basic negotiation qualities" (p. 64). During the semester, they put the pairs of students into an extremely difficult negotiating situation, one that guaranteed initial failure and required persistence and creative thinking to get beyond. As with Dweck's fifth graders, the growth–mind-set students worked better in the postfailure condition: "The more negotiators collectively endorsed an incremental view, the more likely they were to overcome initial failures and construct an agreement that led to an acceptable solution for both parties" (p. 60). The researchers also discovered, as Dweck did with her fifth graders, that student mind-set influenced learning performance more generally. At the end of the semester, they compared the students' final grades in the course with the mind-set attitudes they had expressed on the first day of the semester The result: "The more malleable students believed negotiating ability to be on the first day of class, the higher their final course grade 15 weeks later" (p. 61). The students who saw negotiating skills as something capable of improvement actually did improve their negotiating skills more substantively than those who believed them to be stable. Their attitude toward learning, at least in part, expanded or limited their actual learning.

Outside of specific courses, psychologists Richard Robins and Jennifer Pals looked at how students with different mind-sets performed and did or didn't evolve over the course of their 4 years in college. They measured the mind-sets of more than 500 students at the University of California at Berkeley, asking them to evaluate the accuracy of statements like, "I have a certain ability level, and it is something that I can't do much about," or "I can change the way I act in academic contexts, but I can't change my true ability level." The results of their surveys across the students' 4 years of college show dramatic differences between entity (fixed) and incremental (growth) theorists in almost every aspect of their learning attitudes and behavior. To cite just a few:

- "Entity theorists adopted performance goals, presumably in an effort to prove or document their fixed ability level, whereas Incremental theorists adopted learning goals, presumably in an effort to improve or increase their malleable ability level" (p. 329).
- "Entity theorists blamed their failure on low ability yet explained away their success by attributing it to luck.

Emotionally, they felt more distressed about their academic performance and were less likely to feel determined and inspired, despite performing as well as Incremental theorists" (p. 329).

- "Behaviorally, Entity theorists reported that they give up in challenging situations" (p. 329).

Beyond attitudes and behaviors, the researchers confirmed what Mueller and Dweck (1998) and Kray and Haselhuhn (2007) had found: mind-set affects actual academic performance. As a group, entity theorists in this particular experiment came in to college with an overall higher record of academic achievement than the incremental theorists based on measures like SAT or ACT scores. Yet, despite their weaker record of prior academic achievement, the college grades of the incremental theorists as a group reached up to match those of the entity theorists. The growth–mind-set students had improved their potential and performance over the course of their 4 years, whereas the fixed–mind-set students had remained stable.

To best understand how all of this research will allow you to foster the growth mind-set in your students, and to do so in ways that fit within the framework of small teaching, consider one final study on mind-set, this one a collaborative effort between Dweck and three other researchers (Murphy 2014a). In this case they sought to understand whether organizations, like people, could have mind-sets. To measure this, they distributed mind-set–based surveys to more than 500 employees at seven large corporations. The types of questions they used should look familiar by now: "When it comes to being successful, this company seems to believe that people have a certain amount of talent, and they can't really do much to change it." Two major findings emerged from their analysis of the surveys, both of which are consistent with the research of mind-sets within individuals: organizations did exhibit markedly different mind-sets about natural talents and abilities versus efforts, and growth mind-sets within organizations were associated with a wide range of positive and desirable characteristics. Companies with growth mind-sets, according to one presentation of the research, (a) support more collaboration; (b) encourage innovation and creativity; (c) support employees when they try new things and take measured risk; (d) show fewer unethical behaviors (e.g., cheating, cutting corners); and (e) are overall, more supportive of their employees. In sum, they found that "employees thrive in companies that endorse a growth mindset". This was true of both lower level employees and their supervisors. When I first encountered this research, what struck me most sharply was how the phrases used to describe these results lined up so clearly with what we want for our students: effective collaboration, innovation and creativity, a willingness to try new things and take risks, and academic integrity.

Classrooms are not corporations, but they are organizations of a certain kind. Thus, the mind-set of a classroom—just like the mind-set of an organization—will depend largely on the language and actions of the "supervisor" at the front of the room. The most heartening quality about mind-set research, and the reason it occupies a chapter in this book, is that mind-sets are changeable. Lots of new research is emerging on the power of specific interventions designed to change students' mind-sets; unfortunately, most of the interventions that have been studied and measured involve providing mind-set tutorials or workshops to students outside the classroom, at orientation sessions or other events not associated with specific courses. (For an excellent recent example, see Paunesku, Walton, Romero, Smith, Yeager, & Dweck, 2015.) So I can't offer you a single solution for how to change individual students' mind-sets; that magic bullet has not yet emerged from the research. What I will focus on instead is how to make small teaching interventions to your course design, your feedback on student work, and your communication with students that will enable you to create a growth–mind-set classroom—one that encourages desirable academic qualities like creativity, risk taking, and even integrity. Just as we sought in the motivation chapter to create the conditions for internal motivation to flourish, here, too, we are seeking to create the course and classroom conditions that support and encourage students to adopt the growth mind-set—and in doing so, that contribute to their overall success in college and beyond.

MODELS

Our definition of small teaching activities here expands beyond the level of specific classroom strategies to include tweaks to your course design and small changes in terms of how you communicate with your students.

Reward Growth

To promote a growth mind-set, begin by designing an assessment system that rewards intellectual growth in your students. The very simplest way to do this is to allow students the opportunity to practice and take risks, fail and get feedback, and then try again without having their grades suffer for it. I argued in Chapter 5 that it's essential to give students in your course lots of opportunities to practice whatever skills they will need for your assessments, and we can see now that such opportunities can promote the growth mind-set by allowing students plenty of chances to try and fail and improve. However, a small teaching modification to the design of your assessment system can send this message as well: weigh later assignments in the same sequence more heavily than earlier ones. In other words, if you typically give three exams or three papers and a final (in addition to other types of assignments), don't allot the percentages like this: 15, 15, 15, 25. Work your way up to that final exam, and divide up the percentages in a more graduated fashion: 10, 15, 20, 25. The student who bombs that opening exam still can make a decent grade in the course if the stakes on it are low enough. And all students receive the message that it's OK to fail a little bit in the beginning because they will still have plenty of opportunities to make their grade later in the semester.

An equally effective but perhaps more challenging solution for instructors is to allow students to revise work or retake exams. This year, a colleague of mine instituted a policy of endless revision, which means that students can continue to revise any of their papers throughout the semester as often as they like until they get the grade they receive. I haven't seen this colleague out socially as much as I used to, I suspect because he is now stuck home with endless grading. But you don't have to take this strategy quite as far as my colleague. Start small: select an early exam or paper and offer students at least one opportunity to revise or retake it. I know full well that such a policy will increase your grading load and raise your grade distributions, and I don't make this recommendation lightly. Just note, though, that not every student will take you up on it. Some students will be happy with their grades on the first take, and at least a few others will miss the deadline or not care enough to accept the offer. The point is that making the offer sends a message about the type of classroom you run: in this course, you are communicating to them that you care more about their learning than you do about their specific performance on this particular assignment. If the performance did not match your expectations, try again. What matters is that you learn from it.

Finally, be careful about opening the course with extremely difficult assignments or exams that are designed to show students that you mean business. You certainly might convey that message if you give everyone in the class an F on the first exam.

Growth–mind-set students will sit up and take notice and will double down on their studying for the next exam—just like those effort-praised fifth graders did in Dweck and Mueller's study (1998). But remember that you are likely to have both fixed– and growth–mind-set students in the room with you. An early failure in a new subject will communicate to fixed–mind-set students that they are no good at your discipline and will lead to the kind of debilitating behaviors we saw in the mind-set research. Instead, try to help all of your students along by giving them some early success opportunities. This doesn't mean you have to give a cakewalk first exam; it could mean quizzes that help them feel they are capable of succeeding on the exams, or it could mean short writing assignments that build up to the longer ones.

Give Growth-Language Feedback

Maybe I am the only one who has ever given students ability-based praise, in which case all of you can skip this paragraph and move on to the next model. When I first read Dweck's work, I thought back with horror on all of the times that I had written comments or given oral feedback to students including statements like, "You are a really talented writer!" I meant well, I promise. My intention in those cases was to encourage students whom I saw as possible English majors or even future writers with some praise that would make them feel special and would encourage them to want to write more. Now I recognize how statements like this don't do much for instilling that growth mind-set, and here would be a great place to note that fixed mind-sets hamper students with high valuations of their intelligence as much as they do for students with low valuations of their intelligence. When students believe they are naturally smart and they perceive that quality as a fixed one, they may shy away from challenging tasks because they fear that failure will prove them wrong and that everyone—including themselves—will see that they are not as smart as they thought they were.

These days, as a result of my encounters with growth–mind-set research, I have modified my feedback vocabulary considerably. Statements like "You are a really talented writer" have been excised from my vocabulary and have been replaced with, "Excellent work—you took the strategies we have been working on in class and deployed them beautifully in here," or, "You have obviously worked very hard at your writing, and it shows in this essay." The detailed instructions I might give my students on how to improve for the next time probably look exactly the same; I have just made small shifts in the language I use to frame those instructions. Take a look at the kinds of sentences you speak and write to your students, and note what kind of mind-set those sentences reflect. Are you telling students that they have fixed abilities? Or are you telling them that they can get better?

Growth Talk

Mind-set talk doesn't just happen in feedback on student work; it can color any of our communications with our students, from the syllabus to casual statements in class. Mary Murphy, who did her doctoral research under Dweck and has continued to explore as part of her ongoing research agenda mind-set and its role in classrooms and organizations, asked students to help her identify fixed- and growth–mind-set statements made by professors, the results of which are fascinating (Murphy 2014b). If you had asked me to speculate about what kinds of statements instructors make that instill a fixed mind-set, I would have guessed most of us make comments like the one I made earlier—well-meaning statements of praise for student abilities. I would have been wrong. Consider just some of the following comments that the students in Murphy's research reported hearing from their professors:

- "You either know the formulas and concepts or you don't. You either are the kind of person who has the skills to understand math or you don't."
- "30% of you will fail, 20% of you will get D's. It happens every year, and it will happen this year to you."
- "My neuroscience professor said that he teaches the course like a science course and that if students are not confident about their abilities, he suggests that they transfer to another instructor."

In contrast to these depressing statements, the students in Murphy's study also told her about professors whose growth talk or policies were inspiring to them:

- "I had one math professor who described a student from a previous semester who he said was not naturally good at math; however, he regularly attended office hours and asked questions and ended up getting the highest grade in the class. He told the story to encourage students to ask questions and attend office hours."
- "My professor said the point of doing the work wasn't always the ability or end product, but the process of working on the project and getting better at science."
- "We had no idea how to write a scientific paper, but my class had a 72-hour policy where all students could turn in their paper 72 hours before it was due and the TA would read it and give comments. This helped teach you what you did right, what you did wrong, and how to fix it before it was submitted for a grade."

The easiest way to check your mind-set talk is to review your syllabus, assignment sheets, and other written communication with students and ensure that all of these instill the conviction that students can succeed in your course through hard work, effort, and perseverance. If you seed that talk throughout your written communication with students, eventually—if it has not already—it will appear in your more casual oral communications with students as well.

Promote Success Strategies

One of my teaching-in-higher-education heroes is Joe Hoyle, an accounting professor at the University of Richmond whose work I have profiled both in the *Chronicle of Higher Education* and in a previous book (Lang 2013). Hoyle writes a regular blog on teaching in higher education and has won more teaching awards and accolades than I would care to count. The growth mind-set shines forth in every one of Hoyle's communications with his students, from his syllabus to his feedback. Consider just one example. In the spring, after students have registered for their fall courses, Hoyle sends an e-mail to the students to prepare them for their experience together: "I think that if you will put in a good effort next semester, you will be absolutely amazed by how much you can learn about financial accounting." When students actually arrive at the course in the fall and are handed the syllabus, that initial growth talk is echoed by many more such statements on the syllabus. "You will often hear me say: HOURS EQUAL POINTS," begins one paragraph of the syllabus. "If you don't choose to invest time, you will not do well … You have a lot of ability; if you are willing to invest the time, you will learn an amazing amount and be extremely pleased with what you accomplish" (Hoyle 2012). Although you see the word *ability* in here, you can also see that he turns the notion upside down: everyone has ability, so ability alone won't get you anywhere. Successful students put that ability to *work*.

Beyond the talk students hear from Hoyle, though, they also get something else: concrete advice on *how* to learn and succeed in his courses. I'll give my two favorite examples. First, Hoyle does not limit the growth-minded advice he gives to his students to his own perspective; he also asks students who have earned As in the course to write a letter to future students outlining how they managed it. Hoyle has compiled the best of these comments into a single document that he hands out to each fresh new crop of students. When you look it over, you can see how his choice of comments continues to enforce the power of the growth mind-set in his course:

> DON'T GIVE UP on this class. Don't do it after the first test, after the second test, or right before the final. Just don't do it. I went into the final thinking that I had a very slim chance of making an A, but I tried my hardest to do the best that I possibly could and it paid off! And even if you feel like there is no chance you can do well, go talk with Professor Hoyle. I always left my talks with him with a drive to do better.

Every student statement in the document speaks to the three major points you find in this comment: the importance of working hard; the importance of persevering in the face of challenges in the course; and the importance of taking advantage of the many opportunities Hoyle gives them to better their grades. Consider whether your future students could use a document like this one; getting it started entails nothing more than an e-mail to the students who have earned As in your course asking for a paragraph description of how they succeeded. Most A students will relish an assignment like this.

In addition to enlisting these successful students to give good advice to their peers, Hoyle offers some of this kind of advice himself. Beyond the growth talk, in other words, he talks to them about concrete strategies for how they can learn most effectively in the course. This one, from the syllabus, advises students to join their peers in preclass discussions to prepare themselves for the Socractic-style teaching that they encounter every day in Hoyle's classroom:

> A lot of students like to gather in the atrium 30–45 minutes before my classes just to sit and discuss the handouts. I think that is wonderful. I think that really helps. They always walk into class ready to go. If I could, I would require that. Absolutely!!! However, do me a personal favor. If there are people in the atrium from our class, include everyone in the conversation. Some people are quiet and don't want to butt in. I want everyone in the class to become part of the group. Don't be snooty. You make the move to be friendly. (Hoyle 2012)

The longer you teach, the more you will notice how successful students in your course or your discipline engage in certain actions or have certain habits that enable their success. As you observe those things, why not pass them along to your students in the way Hoyle does here? You can even talk to them about what enabled you to succeed as a learner in your discipline. I have been saying to my students for many years now that my own writing in college improved when I began a practicing a very simple habit: for every paper I had to write, I set myself a personal due date 24 hours before the actual due date. This enabled me to have a full day available for reconsideration and revision. I have seen how the best essays in my classes almost always come from students who practice some version of this habit, and I tell my students that as well. Does every student take this good advice? Obviously not. But talking to them about it helps convey the message that success comes not just from ability but also from planning, strategizing, and working.

PRINCIPLES

One way to brainstorm messages to your students about the growth mindset would be to consider how you have overcome setbacks and failures in your disciplinary research or your teaching. Those of us who have completed advanced degrees will have growth mindsets in our areas of specialty. When you were faced with failure in your teaching or felt stuck in your research, what enabled you to break through? How did you learn to persist? Can you pass those strategies along to your students? As you consider how to inspire your students with such growth mindset talk, keep in mind these three basic principles.

Design for Growth Fostering the growth mind-set begins with the course structure. How can you use that structure to reward students for their effort and give them opportunities to revise and improve their work? And how can you do it in ways that don't require you to sacrifice all of your free time and your sanity? Consider small teaching movements toward the ideal: make one assignment per semester open for revision, or offer one 3-hour office-hours session in which students who have a paper due can bring in a draft and get your feedback. Consider how you are weighting the sequence of your assignments and what your first graded assignment will convey to your students about the prospect of learning and success in your class.

Communicate for Growth Speak to students with growth language in both your formal and informal communications with them. Although this process might begin before the semester launches, if you are like Hoyle, for most of us growth talk begins with the syllabus. What would a growth syllabus look like? How would it help students recognize the value of hard work and effort in your course? And how can growth talk then continue throughout the semester on your assignment sheets, in your postings to the course website, in your conversations with them in class and even in your office?

Feedback for Growth Some part of the feedback we give to students on their work will usually be *summative*, telling them what they did right or wrong that earned them a particular grade. However, some part of it should always be *formative*, telling them how to improve for next time. Pitch that formative feedback in growth language. Let them know what kind of effort they will need to improve on the next assignment, and express your confidence in their ability to do so. Take an extra few seconds to conclude your standard comment on a student's paper with sentences like this: "All of this will require effort on your part, but that effort should really pay off on your next paper."

SMALL TEACHING QUICK TIPS: GROWING

Consider your course and classroom as an organization or social space that has norms, codes of behavior, and other malleable qualities (Howard 2015). Ensure that those norms include a growth mindset through as many small modifications as you can implement.

- Provide early success opportunities through assignment sequencing or assessment design.
- Consider offering some reward for effort or improvement in the course, either through the weighting of your assessments (heavier toward the latter half) or through a portion of the grade set aside for that purpose.
- Provide examples of initial failures or setbacks in your own intellectual journey or in those of famous or recognizable figures in your field to demonstrate that such failures can be overcome.

- Give feedback to students in growth language; convey the message that they are capable of improvement, and offer specific instructions on how to achieve the improvement.
- Ask top students to write letters to future students about how they succeeded in the course; select and pass along the ones that highlight the power of effort and perseverance.
- Include a "Tips for Success in This Course" section on your syllabus, and refer to it throughout the semester.

CONCLUSION

I once presented an overview of the growth and fixed mind-sets and their implications for higher education teaching at a faculty workshop that was being videotaped for instructors on campus who could not attend. Afterward, the man operating the camera came up to me and said, "You know, I don't normally listen to the people who are giving these workshops, but something about that growth–mind-set stuff caught my attention. I've got a story I can tell you about that."

His story went like this.

When he was in high school, his family moved across town to a two-family house. The family in the other half of the house included a young man who was widely recognized as the star athlete in their town. Everyone saw him as a natural wonder, someone who was just born to play sports. After they had lived in the house for a few weeks, the cameraman noticed that this young man spent 4 hours per day working out in the backyard, both exercising and conducting drills related to the various sports he played. The cameraman said his first thought when he observed this kind of dedication, day after day, went something like this: "Boy, people who are such naturally talented athletes sure love to practice their sports!" Then, over the course of many more weeks and months of observing this, he realized that the truth was quite different: the young man was a so-called naturally talented athlete because he spent 4 hours every day practicing his sports. "At that moment," the cameraman said, "I realized what it meant to have a growth mind-set, even if I didn't think about it in those terms."

I like to tell this story at my workshops now because it illustrates perfectly the two essential points of this chapter: first, that the cameraman's initial mind-set completely shaped his interpretation of what he was observing in that backyard; and second, and most important, that his interpretation of his observations changed—but only when his mind-set changed.

Mind-sets are crucial—but mind-sets can change.

We can help.

Chapter 9

Expanding

INTRODUCTION

On a freezing February evening, as the snow from a recent blizzard lay in massive drifts around my campus, I bundled into a small classroom with two dozen students in Professor Cary LeBlanc's upper-level marketing class at Assumption College. I was there to observe an example of what you might describe as big teaching: large-scale, revolutionary, innovative types of courses that completely break from the mold of traditional college and university teaching and that represent the opposite end of the spectrum from small teaching. As class began, I was treated almost immediately to the kind of strategy favored by big teachers like LeBlanc. This was the second class period of the course, a seminar that met for 2.5 hours once per week. During the first class session, LeBlanc had introduced students to the course, given them a draft syllabus, and then put the students in the groups and requested that the groups come to the next class period with suggestions for how they wanted the class to run. Two groups were given the assignment of making changes to the course schedule; another group was asked to look at the assessment scheme; still another focused on how students would communicate with each other and with LeBlanc throughout the semester. The class period I observed began with LeBlanc reminding the students of the purpose of this exercise:

"The intent of the discussion we will have in this particular class is to establish a more comprehensive course, one that builds on the basic foundation of the syllabus, while incorporating student changes to enhance the experience and gain buy-in and commitment." He later noted that he expected responsibility for the course structure to be at an 80–20 percent split; he was responsible for the frame and most of the final decisions, but he wanted at least 20 percent of the final structure to come from them. The presentations and discussion began slowly, as students initially seemed unsure of how much he really expected them to contribute. By the time the class reached the 1-hour mark, though, the conversation had burst into life. Students not only had lots of opinions about how they wanted the course to run but also had thoughtful, interesting, and intelligent suggestions for how to maximize their learning within the broader framework LeBlanc had provided.

Ceding this kind of control of one's course to students constitutes one form of big teaching—but is small potatoes compared with the real big teaching that was happening within LeBlanc's course, the specific subject matter of which was microfinancing. Although it comes in many forms, microfinancing most commonly refers to an economic practice of providing small business loans to individuals in developing economies to help them gain financial independence by starting their own small businesses (Banerjee and Dufflo 2011, pp. 157–181). Targeted toward individuals who normally might not have access to capital, microfinancing programs seek to empower the budding entrepreneurs of developing economies. The low-interest loans offered by such programs may amount to only hundreds of dollars (or less) but could be used to purchase such basic supplies as sewing machines for a collective of rural women who can then begin making and mending clothes. LeBlanc had spent the past several years working toward an innovative way to teach students about microfinancing. A former business professional, with an entrepreneurial streak and experience in a variety of industries, LeBlanc eventually decided that the best way to teach about microfinancing programs would be to enlist his students to create one.

This heady prospect was made possible by the fact that the religious order that sponsors our college has members who live and work in a range of developing economies. LeBlanc reached out to the congregation in the Philippines and asked them whether they could help locate members of their community who could use such microloans and eventually could help administer the funds to those who would receive the loans. LeBlanc's class would then act as the U.S. partner in the program: students would publicize and market the microloan program on our campus and within the local community, which would help the congregation raise the funds to finance the first round of loans; the class would make decisions about loan terms and rates and other logistics of the program; finally, the class would help decide who would receive funding from the applicants in the Philippines. Students would, in short, participate in the process of launching a real-world microloan program and changing the lives of men, women, and children halfway around the world. In the process, they would educate themselves about microfinancing, hone their business skills of development and marketing and communications, and help establish a course that LeBlanc hoped would continue for many years to come.

Now *that's* what I call big teaching. Giving students the opportunity to make a positive difference in the world, immersing them in real-world problems and activities, and forcing them to think creatively and think together about all of the logistics of the course and the program itself—these elements have the potential to create an incredibly powerful learning experience for LeBlanc's students. If you look carefully at almost any institution of higher education in the United States and perhaps even around the world, you will find at least one or two instructors engaged in these kinds of big teaching endeavors, pushing the boundaries of what we can accomplish within the framework of a conventional college course and opening up new pathways for all of us to consider. What you will also find, when you take that careful look at the work of these instructors, is that they have devoted an extraordinary amount of time and effort to these teaching innovations, often funded by internal or external grants or with release time or other forms of financial or professional support. I asked LeBlanc, for example, to send me a one-paragraph summary of the work he had put into the course's development. With apologies, he sent me a two-page, single-spaced document describing the 2-year odyssey of creating the course, from its original conception in 2013 through his trip to the Philippines to visit possible recipients of microloans in winter 2015. Just reading his account of what he had endured and accomplished to establish the course was exhausting.

I have been arguing all throughout this book that you should not *have* to expend that level of time and effort to create powerful learning experiences for your students. The strategies that fall under the umbrella of small teaching can begin enhancing the learning of your students when you step into class tomorrow. I also know, however, that learning and thinking about teaching can be like popping the lid on Pandora's box and that some instructors who start small with retrieval practice or self-explaining or adopting growth language in the classroom will decide that they want to explore further and will want a glimpse down some of the pathways that have been opened up by teachers like LeBlanc. My own trajectory as an instructor has followed that model. I first dipped a toe into the literature on teaching and learning for an eminently practical reason: I wanted to figure out how I could get quiet students to participate more actively in the discussions I was having in class. I read about some great techniques for doing so, but I also discovered lots of other ways to engage students in a classroom besides whole-class discussions. Eventually I began to wonder about the purpose of holding discussions in class and how that connected to the larger purpose of students being in college in the first place. The questions raised by those reflections led me to explore some big teaching alternatives, most recently service learning, about which you will hear more in a moment. The point here is that although teaching innovation can begin small, as I have been arguing throughout this book, it can also expand. In this final chapter, then, we will focus on expanding: expanding your own view of what student learning might look like in your classroom and how you might design and conduct your courses. We will accomplish this by considering three big teaching pathways that strike me as logical extensions of what we have considered thus far and that I believe have staying power in the fast-changing landscape of higher education teaching and learning.

MODELS, PRINCIPLES, AND RESOURCES

Since each of the following models represents an entirely different approach to pedagogy, the principles will appear just after the models rather than in a separate final section. Following the three major models and principles, you'll find suggestions for resources that will help you continue to expand your thinking about teaching big and small.

Activity-Based Learning

An outstanding source of pathways to big (and small) teaching is the ABLConnect database at Harvard University (http://ablconnect.harvard.edu), which serves as a gathering place of research, examples, and ideas for pedagogical innovation in higher education. ABLConnect distinguishes between two types of learning activities collected within its searchable database: *active learning*, a term with which you are likely familiar and that would cover just about every teaching strategy described in this book; and *activity-based learning*, which "involves fieldwork, public service, community-based research and internships in conjunction with in-class work" (ABLConnect). Cary LeBlanc's class constitutes an intensive example of an activity-based learning course. Such courses identify a large-scale activity that somehow connects to the discipline, the completion of which will require students to gain the knowledge and skills to be taught in the course. In LeBlanc's course, the creation and administration of the microloan program would constitute that large-scale activity. To do that, however, the students have to study marketing and development principles that will help them understand how to raise funds for the program. To accomplish *that* objective, they are engaging with course readings, meeting with development professionals both in and outside of class who will share their expertise with the students, and of course working under the guidance of LeBlanc, who will coach them and provide feedback and assess them along the way. The activity around which LeBlanc built the course requires them to master the core knowledge and skills of the discipline.

Activity-based learning does not have to extend throughout the entire semester, though. In my creative nonfiction course, an upper-level writing seminar, I have had students engage in an activity-based learning exercise that lasts around a week. It happens when we are working in the unit of the course that is dedicated to writing about places, with the travel essay as our model. In small groups, the students are charged with visiting some hidden places on campus—places that students might not normally think to go. They bring their notes from these visits in class, and we spend two class periods coauthoring, as a class, an essay on the hidden places on our campus for the college newspaper. I contact the editor beforehand to arrange for publication of the piece, which means that from the start of this exercise the students know that their work will appear in print and that we have a deadline to meet. We use a shared Google doc to create the jointly authored essay, with each group submitting its section and then all of us editing it together to create a smooth, consistent style. The energy and interest that I observe during those two class periods is enough to convince me of the power of activity-based learning and to continue to reflect on how it might find a place in my classes. Creating this activity was no 2-year odyssey for me; it took only an e-mail to the editor of the newspaper, a little bit of technological work to create and manage the Google doc, and a single week's worth of class time.

One connection you can see between both LeBlanc's course and my much briefer example is that our activities extended the work of students out of the confines of our classroom and into a more public space: LeBlanc's students are giving loans to real people, not connected with the college, and my students are writing for the entire campus audience. My intuitive sense is that if you can find an activity that will require students to prepare or showcase their work for a public audience, this will help them see connections between your discipline and your course and the world around them. This can help boost motivation by invoking larger, more public purposes for their course work. But creating such public connections is not a requirement of activity-based learning. You could very well create an activity that students completed entirely within the course—and even within a single class session. The ABLConnect site features an excellent example of such an activity from a course on ancient Mesoamerican civilizations from the University of Oklahoma, in which the students learned about the challenges of food gathering and preparation in ancient civilizations by preparing tortillas and hot chocolate using traditional (i.e., long and time-consuming) methods in a single class period. The end product didn't make it out of the class, as instructor Christine Warinner noted: "They ate the result of their labors." However, they both thoroughly enjoyed the activity and learned an important lesson from it: "Students were surprised by how hard it is to grind maize into masa, and that helped put into perspective the gendered labor of ancient Mesoamerica, in which women were expected to grind maize for many hours every day" (ABLConnect). So activity-based learning can encompass small, internal, single-class activities like this one as easily as it can encompass large-scale projects like the creation of a microloan program in the Philippines.

Principle Here is a quick and easy principle for envisioning activity-based learning experiences for your students: ask them to do whatever people do outside of your class in your discipline or with the specific content and skills you are teaching them. Some writers use placed-based skills to write travel essays for newspapers and magazines, so that's what I asked of my students; some marketing professionals create campaigns to inform people and open their wallets, so that's what LeBlanc's students did; some anthropologists seek to understand the real living conditions of ancient people, so that's what Warinner's students did. Look *outside* the course for inspiration on what you could bring back *into* the course. To jumpstart your thinking on activity-based learning, visit the ABLConnect website, or see John Bean's (2011) wonderful book *Engaging Ideas: The Professional's Guide to Integrating Writing, Critical Thinking, and Active Learning in the Classroom* for plenty of excellent examples.

Service Learning

Service learning is the generous cousin of activity-based learning and represents a pathway that I believe more and more instructors should consider for their courses. For me, service learning helps provide a convincing answer to an increasingly difficult question that students and parents and the public are asking those of us who still teach on brick-and-mortar campuses: in the age of information and connection, with the costs of traditional colleges and universities soaring endlessly out of sight, why are we still asking students to come learn on our campuses? What special benefits do students gain from sitting in your classes and living on your campus that they cannot obtain from a hacked or DIY education obtained at a fraction of the cost? One of the best—if not the best—answers we can provide to that question is that college and university campuses can provide positive contributions to the local, regional, and global communities in which they are situated. College faculty, staff, and students constitute an incredibly rich resource of intellectual capital and youthful energy, and that combination has tremendous potential to make a positive difference to the world—not just after the students graduate but also while they are on campus. Of course, the main purpose of college remains educating its students, but if it can accomplish that purpose while also providing valuable services to the community, why not? And what if it turned out that providing valuable services to the community turned out to be one of the most effective ways of educating students? We have seen already how the idea of a self-transcendent purpose to learning can prove a powerful source of motivation to students; service learning helps inspire such self-transcendent motivation in college and university courses.

Studies of community service learning have demonstrated that student benefit dramatically in a variety of ways from putting their learning in context of service to the community. Dan Butin, in the introduction to a special issue of the *International Journal of Teaching and Learning in Higher Education* (2006), provided a nice overview of the many potential benefits of the approach:

> By linking theory with practice and classrooms with communities, service learning provides real-world exposure and engagement with meaningful local and global issues through concrete and ameliorative practices. An ever-expanding body of research validates the positive impact of service learning upon a host of academic, social, and cultural variables. Service learning increases youth's civic knowledge and political engagement, strengthens openness to diversity and difference, and promotes a better and deeper understanding of course content.... Such results appear to be sustained even years after the actual service learning has occurred. (p. 1)

Who wouldn't want these outcomes for their students? I have experimented with service learning in two separate courses now and have seen some of these outcomes in my own students. It hasn't been perfect, as I am still feeling my way through the logistics—a point that is probably true with any big teaching initiative and is one of the reasons that big teaching transformations can seem intimidating to instructors. You can almost guarantee a semester or two of feeling your way through it, waiting for the positive outcomes described by Butin to emerge.

Still, the results I have seen have been positive enough that I will be continuing down this pathway in the future—as are many instructors on my own campus and across the country. Although there are numerous possible models for designing courses with service learning, two basic ones will help give you a sense of what service learning typically entails. In both cases, it should go without saying that the service activity connects to some integral component of the course. In this way the students are learning content and developing skills both in their preparation for their service, in the practicing of it, and in their analysis of it and reflections on it afterward. The first model resembles activity-based learning in that students spend class time preparing for some large-scale event or activity—the primary difference being that this activity serves the community in some way. So students in a course on community politics might volunteer together at a Habitat for Humanity build site one weekend, for example, or participate in a daylong clean-up of a local park. Students in a special education course might work with a local school to run a community outreach and educational event for students with disabilities. In the second model, students are instead required to complete a specific number of community service hours with local organizations (selected by the instructors as relevant to the course content) as part of their required course work. The students complete these hours throughout the semester on their own. Those students in the community politics course, in this model, would be required to complete 15 hours of service with a local organization relevant to the course; the students in the education course would complete their hours volunteering at the after-school tutoring sessions.

In both cases, and in all types of community service learning, what matters the most is that class time and course assessments are tied to the service work. The service work cannot simply be an add-on to the regular course content, vaguely tied to it but not linked to it in any substantive way. If you want to encourage students to do community service, send them to the local office on campus that provides volunteer opportunities for your students. If you want to use community service learning, you have to be willing to fold it meaningfully into your course. Students should have the opportunity to analyze and reflect on their service through journals or class discussions; they should be assessed on their analysis and reflections (not necessarily their service) through formal papers or presentations or other types of assignments, and they should read or study material related to the organizations you are serving or the larger social problems those organizations seek to address. The most important word in community service learning is *learning*, so that has to remain at the center of your course. As long as you are following that prescription, service learning strikes me as a second big teaching innovation that has the power to inspire and motivate students and that helps both students and outside constituents—parents, politicians, the public at large—see deeper value in the colleges and universities in their towns.

Principle Attempting to launch a service-learning course on your own can be an intimidating prospect, but the chances are very slim that you will have to go it on your own. As the popularity of service learning has been waxing in higher education, many campuses now have designated offices or individuals who can help instructors with the logistics of connecting their students to local community organizations that need help. Start your explorations with that office or that person. But even if such an office doesn't exist on your campus, the chances are excellent that at least one or more of your colleagues teaches with this model already. Find this colleague, buy her a coffee, and learn whatever you can before you begin to experiment with your own classes. If you would rather get started with some reading, *Service Learning Essentials: Questions, Answers, and Lessons Learning* (2014) will give you a good overview of the opportunities and challenges.

Games and Simulations

In the mid-1990s Mark Carnes was teaching history at Barnard College—and by all accounts doing an excellent job of it. At the conclusion of one semester, as he tried to spark a discussion of Plato's *Republic* with a group of listless students, he decided that something was missing from his classes. He recounted the story in his book *Minds on Fire: How Role-Immersion Games Can Transform College* (2014). "Within a week the semester would be over," he thought to himself after the class concluded, "and they would be gone. Had the class meant anything to them? To me?" (p. 18). After the winter break, he sent an e-mail to students in the class asking them to come visit him in his office; he wanted to ask them if they could help him identify the missing spark that would have fueled more energetic discussions, more commitment to the class. When one student professed in bewilderment that Carnes's class was her favorite class that semester, he responded with exasperation: "You were bored! I was bored! You could *feel* the boredom in the room!" The girl's response startled Carnes: "But all classes are sorta boring. Yours was less boring than most" (pp. 18–19). In the wake of that conversation, Carnes spent the next several years developing a revolutionary new approach to higher education pedagogy called Reacting to the Past. Born from Carnes's classroom experiments, the approach has been spreading quickly on college and university campuses in the United States, with instructors at now more than 300 institutions who are using Reacting games in their courses.

Reacting to the Past consists of role-immersion games in which students are put into the place of historical actors at key moments of crisis or transition in human history and, under the watchful eye of the instructor, play out their own version of those historical events to some final conclusion. For example, students might assume the roles of the different political parties who had a stake in creating an independent India after the British announced they would withdraw from the country they had governed as a colonial power for so many years. Or they might assume the roles of the different factions that sought to create a constitution for

France in the wake of the French Revolution. Students prepare to take on these roles within complex historical contexts by doing extensive readings in published or working game books, which gather together primary and secondary documents that provide them with the necessary historical background; many students become so engaged by the games, though, that they conduct their own extensive research outside of the game books. The games can last anywhere from 3 to 6 weeks, which means two can be accommodated in a semester, although recently the Reacting consortium has been working on brief, chapter-length games that can take place during a single week or even a class period.

One of the most distinctive features of the games is that the "history" that plays out within them is open; all of the historical contexts and documents are real ones, but what happens in the game does not have to match what happened in the real world. Students in the games are competitors who have objectives that they must meet to turn the outcome toward their side. In the game devoted to India on the eve of independence from Britain's colonial presence, for example, some of the players want a united India; some of them want an India partitioned into Hindu and Muslim states; others want even less likely alternatives. All the students are given role sheets that fully describe their character (usually a real historical figure, but sometimes imagined or composite characters are used) and that describe what they must accomplish to win the game. A Hindu nationalist, for example, will win the India game if he can convince his fellow Indians to maintain a united India after the British have withdrawn; a Muslim nationalist will win if he can convince the group to create a separate Muslim state. After the students have prepared for their roles with extensive reading and research, they spend class time making speeches, politicking, plotting, and engaging in any other activity that will help them achieve their objectives. The instructor's role is to observe, assess, and occasionally—in very limited ways—intervene to keep the game on track. Grading stems from the written and oral work of the students, such as the speeches they write and deliver during class sessions.

Every year the Reacting consortium hosts a conference that interested or participating instructors can attend to learn how to teach with the games, preview new games in development, and share teaching ideas and strategies with each other. I had the opportunity to attend the conference one year and to play a 2-day version of one of the games as a student. It was without a doubt one of the most charged and fascinating experiences of my life. For better or worse, we humans seem to find competition a motivating factor, and the games are centered on charged historical moments that enable the students to read and argue about deep and widespread human experiences. After my experience at the conference, I spent some time interviewing Kurt Squire, professor of digital media in curriculum and instruction and games researcher at the University of Wisconsin, trying to understand how they sparked the kind of deep learning I experienced at the conference. "Games are a good model for introducing a topic and raising interest," Squire told me, "because they situate content for learners so that they understand why it's relevant" (Lang, 2014). The games accomplish that by establishing immediate goals that players can attain only by learning and applying course content. (Recollect the importance of goals and purpose to learning, as we saw in Chapter 7.) We often spend weeks throwing content at our students, and perhaps by the end of the semester we hope to have convinced them that what they have learned is relevant beyond the classroom. In a simulation game, by contrast, you are confronted immediately with the realization that what you are learning will help achieve a goal. Even though the winners of a Reacting game usually earn no substantive prize for achieving that goal—many instructors will offer bonus points to the winners, but assessment largely depends on individual efforts—the competitive nature of the games seems to be enough to spark and stimulate the interest and the effort of students.

As I noted in the introduction to the book, Reacting is a big teaching approach in one very important aspect: it requires a substantial investment of time and energy by an instructor to learn how to run games and to use them for the first several times. Just like activity-based learning, however, opportunities exist for using games and simulations outside this very specific and extensive framework. Any instructor can incorporate simulations into a classroom—or even into online courses or in assignments—in a range of possible forms, within any possible time frame. Squire's Games+Learning+Society institute at the University of Wisconsin offers an excellent resource for instructors who want to understand more clearly how games and simulations more generally intersect with learning and who would like to explore further the possibility of using them in their teaching. Consider as well exploring the Reacting consortium website (https://reacting.barnard.edu/), where you can find information on the variety of available Reacting games. If games and simulations strike you as a big teaching initiative that might find a place into your classroom, these represent two excellent starting points to learn more and consider possibilities.

Principle Because Reacting has been around for 2 decades now and the published games have been road-tested by hundreds of instructors in a range of contexts from research universities to community colleges, your first and easiest pathway to games and simulations would be to check the consortium website to see if a game exists that will work for your course. If not, you can find simulations in almost any discipline through basic searches. Some—like Sniffy the Virtual Rat, which gives psychology students a virtual laboratory experience—will require you (or your students) to spend some money; others are free, like Budget

Hero, which challenges students to master the complexities of the federal budget. In short, don't attempt to invent the wheel with simulations in your discipline; chances are pretty good that some exist already. To get started with Reacting to the Past, first check out Carnes's *Minds on Fire* (2014), and then attend the annual conference held each June on Barnard's campus in New York City.

Resources

In keeping with the spirit of the book, I will make three small recommendations for how to expand your vision as a teacher after finishing this book. Make a commitment to read one additional book on teaching and learning this year (and at least one per year after that), to consult at least one higher education Web source per week (or sign up for an e-mail list that will link you to such a site), and to create a personal learning network on Twitter with your favorite teaching experts. Here are five suggestions in each category to get you started.

Books: The field of teaching and learning in higher education has been growing exponentially in recent years, with many dozens of new books appearing every year. Keep your eye on the higher education catalogues of Jossey-Bass, Harvard University Press, the University of Chicago Press, and Stylus for major new titles in the field.

· *What the Best College Teachers Do* (Bain, 2004). Ken Bain's elegantly written analysis of highly effective college teachers remains for me the first book that all college teachers, new and experienced, should read at some point during their careers.
· *Make It Stick: The Science of Successful Learning* (Brown, Roedger, and McDaniel, 2014). The most authoritative, expertly

researched, and well-written book available on how people learn and what it means for us as teachers (and learners).

- *How Learning Works: 7 Research-Based Principles for Smart Teaching* (Ambrose, Bridges, DiPietro, Lovett, and Norman, 2010). The title says it all. Aimed at college and university instructors, a clear and well-researched overview of what college teachers should know about topics like motivation, feedback, and student intellectual development.
- *Mindset: The New Psychology of Success* (Dweck, 2006). If you were interested in the research presented in Chapter 8 on the growth mind-set, this is the book for you. This is Dweck's overview of the role mind-set plays in shaping many aspects of our lives.
- *Why Don't Students Like School* (Willingham, 2008). Although Willingham's book articulates its audience as K–12 teachers, this college instructor found in it as much new and useful and fascinating information about learning and teaching to merit my highly recommending it to college and university instructors as well.

Web Resources: I have difficulty finding the time for books outside of my field during the semester, so throughout the academic year I rely on shorter resources like the ones below. Generally I spend the first ten or fifteen minutes of my workday paging through resources like these, and will listen to the podcast while I am running errands, exercising, or doing housework.

- *ABLConnect*: http://ablconnect.harvard.edu/ This website, from Harvard University, offers an ever-growing compendium of concrete strategies for active and activity-based learning.
- *Pedagogy Unbound*: http://www.pedagogyunbound.com A similar site, the self-description of which promises to help you "Discover practical tips for this semester." Founder David

Gooblar also writes a regular column, of the same title, in the *Chronicle of Higher Education.*

· *Faculty Focus:* http://www.facultyfocus.com A free service offered by Magna Publications, this site offers summaries of new research or ideas, as well as original contributions from instructors on teaching tips that work. You can sign up for an e-mail list or just check in on a weekly basis.
· *Chronicle of Higher Education*: http://chronicle.com In recent years the *Chronicle* has been featuring more and more essays by instructors on teaching, from my own monthly *On Course* column to the excellent ideas and suggestions of the ProfHackers group. Sign up for the daily free digest and click through to one or two interesting-looking articles per week.
· *Podcast: Teaching in Higher Ed*: http://teachinginhighered.com/episodes/ Each week Bonni Stachowiak speaks with an author, innovator, or researcher in higher education teaching and learning and shares the 30–40 minutes interview on her Podcast.

Twitter: I highly recommend the use of Twitter to establish a personal learning network that will connect you to people who are doing interesting things in college and university classrooms around the world. To get your network started, follow these frequent posters, excellent writers, and thoughtful instructors or faculty development experts:

· **@DerekBruff:** Derek Bruff, director of the Center for Teaching at Vanderbilt University and author of *Teaching with Classroom Response Systems* (2009)
· **@SaRoseCav:** Sarah Cavanagh, associate professor of psychology and director of the Laboratory for Cognitive and Affective Science at Assumption College, author of *The Spark of Learning: Energizing the College Classroom with the Science of Emotion* (2016)

- **@josebowen:** Jose Bowen, president of Goucher College and author of *Teaching Naked: How Moving Technology Out of Your Classroom Will Improve Student Learning* (2012)
- **@MDMichelleMiller:** Michelle Miller, professor of psychology and director of the First-Year Learning Initiative at Northern Arizona University, author of *Minds Online: Teaching with Technology* (2014)
- **@teachprof:** The Twitter feed of *The Teaching Professor*, an excellent newsletter, with frequent posts on new research and teaching tips for college and university professors.

Finally, you can also join the conversation about small teaching and continue to receive new ideas and updates by connecting with me at @LangOnCourse and using the hashtag #SmallTeaching to link other instructors to new ideas, resources, and questions.

SMALL TEACHING QUICK TIPS: EXPANDING

My experience speaking with faculty audiences for the past dozen years has been that most of us like our work, believe in what we do, and want to improve. As in every field, though, the sheer number of resources available to us can be overwhelming. Don't imagine you need to master this body of research; just aim to keep yourself thinking.

- Commit to reading at least one new book on teaching and learning every year.
- Subscribe to an e-mail list from *Faculty Focus* or *Chronicle of Higher Education* or a similar site and read one or two articles per week that will keep you informed of new research in higher education.

- Create a personal learning network on Twitter; use hashtags such as #highered, #edutech, #edchat, #teaching, and #learning to find new peers with whom to connect.
- Attend a conference on teaching and learning in higher education to expand your vision even further. Most disciplines have dedicated conferences in their fields; if your discipline does not, try one of the major general conferences such as The Teaching Professor or the Lilly Conference on College and University Teaching.
- Attend events on your campus sponsored by your local faculty development center (which might go under the name of Center for Teaching Excellence, or Center for Teaching and Learning, or some other variation). You'll find both expert help and like-minded colleagues there.

CONCLUSION

I want to conclude this chapter by telling you about an exchange that occurred while I was observing LeBlanc's microfinancing course. Remember that LeBlanc had given students the responsibility and opportunity to provide him feedback on his syllabus, including his assessments and grading policies. When it came time for the group that had been assigned to critique the grading policies to make their recommendations, they essentially argued for tweaking the percentages that LeBlanc had allotted to the different assessment activities, such as a personal reflection paper or course participation. One of their specific recommendations along these lines was to reduce the percentage of the course points allotted for two major exams. In response to this recommendation, some students raised their hands and said that they didn't think the course really needed exams at all. "A course like this is really more about developing our creativity and learning how to do this project, not about memorizing information," one student said. After several comments like this, through which I was biting my tongue very hard, a student who had been quiet for the first part of class finally spoke up. "But actually," she said, "we probably *need* tests or quizzes to help us make sure we know the information really well. After all, if we're like meeting with a bunch of potential donors and they start asking us questions about how microfinancing works, we don't want to sit there and not know how to respond. We have to really know our stuff. The tests or quizzes will help make sure everybody learns what we need to know to do our jobs in the course."

Bingo.

As that perceptive student was rightly articulating, even big teachers need to think about small teaching—to help their students master course content while they are inspiring them with creative course designs. During one of the first times I presented the material of this book to a faculty audience, a generally receptive discussion period concluded with a comment from a woman who was having none of it. "Small teaching isn't enough for me," she said. "I want big changes in higher education right now." She may have been surprised at my response: I love big changes. The work of instructors like LeBlanc and Carnes helps all of us in higher education blaze new pathways, and can provide powerful and unforgettable learning experiences for our students. The mistake in her objection was thinking that small teaching precludes or even conflicts with big teaching. In fact, I would argue, the small teaching strategies recommended in this book can form a part of the teaching and learning arsenal of any college or university classroom, from traditional lectures to the most innovative teaching and learning environment we can dream up. Courses like LeBlanc's, just like courses in service learning or courses run with games and simulations, will benefit from small teaching strategies as much as courses that run along more conventional pedagogical lines.

And it may even be the case that if we want the instructor down the hall to consider big changes the best thing we can do for him is to help him make a small change or two. I hope you find courses like LeBlanc's as fascinating and promising as I do. But perhaps you find yourself intimidated by the prospect of running your courses through the revolutionary wringer or wondering how in the world such innovation could make sense in light of all of the responsibilities you bear for teaching certain skills or covering certain content or preparing students for this or that future exam. Don't despair. LeBlanc, like almost any big teacher you have ever heard about, once began where you might be now. Whatever change you are hoping to make to your teaching—from livening up your lectures or increasing participation in your discussions to running better group work sessions or ceding the syllabus to your students or loaning money to future entrepreneurs in the rural outskirts of Manila—you can still reach your objective by making those changes one small (teaching) step at a time.

Conclusion: Beginning

The ultimate aim of this book has been to convince you that you can create powerful learning for your students through the small, everyday decisions you make in designing your courses, engaging in classroom practice, communicating with your students, and addressing any challenges that arise. Even if you find that none of the specific strategies mentioned in this book work for you, I still hope that you will have been convinced that small steps can make a big difference. If you are an instructor, take the models and principles that I have described in this book and adapt them into your courses; if they don't fit, use them instead as inspiration to create your own small teaching strategies. Make an effort to measure the effects of changes that you implement so you can understand how to improve them or when to abandon them if they are not working. You can find plenty of excellent means of measuring the learning of your students, and the effectiveness of specific teaching techniques, in Angelo and Cross's now classic (and still excellent) *Classroom Assessment Techniques* (Angelo and Cross 1993). You can also use quick midterm surveys and end-of-course evaluations for measurement purposes. Linda Nelson's *Teaching at Its Best* contains an excellent overview chapter on documenting and measuring the effectiveness of your teaching with such methods (Nelson 2010).

The best aid, though, to help you initiate and gauge the success of new teaching techniques may be right on your campus, in the form of your center for teaching excellence, center for teaching and learning, or whatever other name it might be called.

There you are likely to find someone who will be thrilled to hear that you are trying new strategies to boost student learning in your courses, who has plenty of experience in implementing and measuring teaching effectiveness, and who will be very glad to assist you at both ends of the process. If you are one of those faculty development professionals, I hope you can use the small teaching framework as a way to gather faculty together and work with them to brainstorm new ways to create powerful learning for students on your campus. What are the common challenges that faculty on your campus are facing right now? Can small thinking, like small teaching, lead to new solutions to those problems? For both instructors and faculty development professionals, when you find something that works, write about it in your blog or post a link on Twitter or submit an essay about it to the *Chronicle* or *Faculty Focus* or present about it at the teaching and learning conference in your field. Let the rest of us know.

For now, you probably have class tomorrow morning, or at least within the next week. Think about the first 5 minutes of that next class period. You could give students a little retrieval practice by spending those opening minutes asking them to answer some questions, either orally or in writing, about the material you covered in the last class or about the reading they completed for homework. You could prepare them for the day's content by asking them to speculate or make a prediction about a problem you will be presenting in your opening mini lecture. You could throw up a fascinating image and ask them to wonder about it. Or perhaps you have to cover a large amount of material with a lecture, but now you want to start it with a story or a question rather than an answer, something that will engage their attention and leave them a little bit puzzled before you provide them with the content they will need to come up with the answer. Perhaps you will even get to class 5 minutes early and make an effort to engage in some informal discussion with a student who has not spoken in class this semester and who just might benefit from some quick social interaction with her instructor.

You also have class next semester. How can you use theories of prediction or pretesting to create an opening-day activity that will activate the prior knowledge of your students and prepare them for learning? How can you ensure that students will continually cycle back to the material they have already learned, to take advantage of the learning power of spacing and interleaving? How can you elicit self-explanations from students when they are engaged in practicing the skills you will test them on? Where might a day spent on the Minute Thesis game pack the most learning punch for your students? What about your written communications with them? Can you revise the language of your syllabus to include recommendations on how students will succeed in the course? Will you modify the language you use when you give feedback to your students to ensure that it promotes a growth mind-set? And how can you let students know about the ways practitioners in your field are making the world a better place—and the ways they might do so someday as well?

Finally, you have a teaching career ahead of you, however long or short that might be at this point in your life. You could continue to explore and experiment with small teaching strategies for another 20 or 30 years and probably still not exhaust the possibilities. Perhaps over time you will recognize that students in your introductory and survey courses need more retrieval practice and motivational talk, whereas students in your upper-level seminars really need more connecting and growth mind-set feedback. Perhaps this notion of a growth mind-set has opened up new ways for you to think about yourself as a teacher, and now you wish to dig into some of the books that I have referenced and recommended in these pages. Or maybe you will push yourself further and explore alternative pedagogies like service learning or Reacting to the Past. If you have been inspired even more deeply, perhaps you will gather a group of colleagues together to share your best ideas for small teaching and learn from one another in addition to learning from the literature on teaching and learning in higher education. The prospects can be as wide or narrow as you wish.

Most important, you have class tomorrow morning.

How will you begin?

Works Cited

ABLConnect. (2015). Harvard University. http://ablconnect.harvard.edu.

Ambrose, S., Bridges, M., DiPietro, M., Lovett, M., & Norman, M. (2010). *How learning works: 7 research-based principles for smart teaching*. San Francisco, CA: Jossey-Bass.

Ambrose, S. A., & Lovett, M. C. (2014). Prior knowledge is more than content: Skills and beliefs also impact learning. In V. A. Benassi, C. E. Overson, & C. M. Hakala (Eds.), *Applying science of learning in education: Infusing pyschological science into the curriculum* (pp. 7–19). Retrieved from http://www.teachpsych.org/Resources/Documents/ebooks/asle2014.pdf

Anderson, L., et al. (2000). *A taxonomy for learning, teaching, and assessing: A revision of Bloom's taxonomy of educational objectives*. New York, NY: Pearson.

Angelo, T. A., & Cross, K. P. (1993). *Classroom assessment techniques: A handbook for college teachers*. San Francisco, CA: Jossey-Bass.

Atkinson, R. K., Renkl, A., & Merrill, M. M. (2003). Transitioning from studying examples to solving problems: Effects of self-explanation prompts and fading worked-out steps. *Journal of Educational Psychology, 95*(4), 774–783.

Bain, K. (2004). *What the best college teachers do*. Cambridge, MA: Harvard University Press.

Banerjee, A., & Duflo, E. (2011). *Poor Economics: A Radical Rethinking of the Way to Fight Global Poverty*. New York, NY: PublicAffairs.

Banning, M. (2004). The think aloud approach as an educational tool to develop and assess clinical reasoning in undergraduate students. *Nurse Education Today, 28*, 8–14.

Bean, J. C. (2011). *Engaging ideas: The professor's guide to integrating writing, critical thinking, and active learning in the classroom.* San Francisco, CA: Jossey-Bass.

Blazer, A. (2014). Student summaries of class sessions. *Teaching Theology and Religion, 17*(4), 344.

Bloom, K. C., & Shuell, T. J. (1981). Effects of massed and distributed practice on the learning and retention of second-language vocabulary. *Journal of Educational Research, 74*(4), 245–248.

Bowen, J. (2012). *Teaching naked: How moving technology out of your college classroom will improve student learning.*. San Francisco, CA: Jossey-Bass.

Brown, P. C., Roediger, H. L., & McDaniel, M. A. (2014). *Make it stick: The science of successful learning.* Cambridge, MA: Harvard University Press.

Bruff, D. (2009). *Teaching with classroom response systems: Creative active learning environments.* San Francisco, CA: Jossey-Bass.

Butin, D. (2006). Future directions for service learning in higher education. *International Journal of Teaching and Learning in Higher Education, 18*(1), 1–4.

Carey, B. (2014a). *How we learn: The surprising truth about when, where, and why it happens.* New York, NY: Random House.

Carey, B. (2014b, September 4). Why flunking exams is actually a good thing. *New York Times.* http://www.nytimes.com/2014/09/07/magazine/why-flunking-exams-is-actually-a-good-thing.html

Carnes, M. (2014). *Minds on fire: How role-immersion games transform college.* Cambridge, MA: Harvard University Press.

Carpenter, S. K., & Mueller, F. E. (2013). The effects of interleaving versus blocking on foreign language pronunciation learning. *Memory and Cognition, 41*(5), 671–682.

Cavanagh, Sarah. (2016). *The spark of learning: Energizing the college classroom with the science of emotion.* Morgantown, WV: West Virginia University Press.

Chambliss, D. F., & Takacs, C. J. (2014). *How college works.* Cambridge, MA: Harvard University Press.

Chi, M. T. H., Bassok, M., Lewis, M. W., Reimann, P., & Glaser, R. (1989). Self-explanations: How students study and use examples in learning to solve problems. *Cognitive Science, 13*, 145–182.

Chi, M. T. H., DeLeeuw, N., Chiu, M.-H., & LaVancher, C. (1994). Eliciting self-explanations improves understanding. *Cognitive Science, 18*, 439–477.

Chiu, J., & Chi, M. T. H. (2014). Supporting self-explanation in the classroom. In V. A. Benassi, C. E. Overson, & C. M. Hakala (Eds.), *Applying science of learning in education: Infusing pyschological science into the curriculum.* (pp. 91–103). Retrieved from http://www.teachpsych.org/Resources/Documents/ebooks/asle2014.pdf

Cornelius, T. L., & Owen-DeSchryver, J. (2008). Differential effects of full and partial notes on learning outcomes and attendance. *Teaching of Psychology, 35*, 6–12.

Dweck, C. (2008). *Mindset: The new psychology of success.* New York, NY: Ballantine.

Flipped classroom model shows proven progress in addressing broken educational experience in U.S. (2013, November 9). *Sonic Foundry.* http://www.sonicfoundry.com/press-release/flipped-classroom-model-shows-proven-progress-addressing-broken-educational-experience

Gregory, S. (2014a, October 29). Dynasty! The San Francisco Giants win it all. *Time.*

Gregory, S. (2014b, October 15). The Kansas City Royals are the future of baseball. *Time.*

Howard, J. (2015). *Discussion in the college classroom: Getting your students engaged and participating in person and online..* San Francisco, CA: Jossey-Bass.

Hoyle, J. (2012, June 3). How to make an A. E-mail to author.

Jacoby, B., & Howard, J. (2014). *Service-learning essentials: Questions, answers, and lessons learned.* San Francisco, CA: Jossey-Bass.

Khanna, M. M., Badura Brack, A. S., & Finken, L. L. (2013). Short- and long-term effects of cumulative finals on student learning. *Teaching of Psychology, 40*(3), 175–182.

Kornell, N., Jenson Hayes, M., & Bjork, R. A. (2009). Unsuccessful retrieval attempts enhance subsequent learning. *Journal of Experimental Psychology: Learning, Memory, and Cognition, 35*(4), 989–998.

Kray, L. J., & Haselhuhn, M. P. (2007). Implicit negotiation beliefs and performance: Experimental and longitudinal evidence. *Journal of Personality and Social Psychology, 93*(1), 49–64.

Lang, J. (2013). *Cheating lessons: Learning from academic dishonesty.* Cambridge, MA: Harvard University Press.

Lang, J. (2014, August 25). How students learn from games. *Chronicle of Higher Education.* Retrieved from http://chronicle.com/article/How-Students-Learn-From-Games/148445/

Langer, E. J. (1997). *The power of mindful learning.* Cambridge, MA: DaCapo.

Miller, M. (2011). What college teachers should know about memory: A perspective from cognitive psychology. *College Teaching, 59,* 117–122.

Miller, M. (2014). *Minds online: Teaching effectively with technology.* Cambridge, MA: Harvard University Press.

Morris, P., Gruneberg, M., Sykes, R., and Merrick, A. (1981). Football knowledge and the acquisition of new results. *British Journal of Psychology, 72*(4), 479–483.

Mueller, C. M., & Dweck, C. S. (1998). Praise for intelligence can undermine children's motivation and performance. *Journal of Personality and Social Psychology, 75*(1), 33–52.

Murphy, M. (2014a, October 16). A study of mindsets in organizations. Indiana State University.

Murphy, M. (2014b, October 15). How students perceive faculty mindsets. E-mail to the author.

Nelson, L. (2010). *Teaching at its best: A research-based resource for college instructors.* (5th ed.). San Francisco: Jossey-Bass.

Ogan, A., Aleven, V., & Jones, C. (2009). Advancing development of intercultural competence through supporting predictions in narrative video. *International Journal of Artificial Intelligence in Education, 19*(3), 267–288.

Orwell, G. (1986). *A clergyman's daughter*. London, UK: Penguin Books.

Orwell, G. (1968). My country right or left: 1940–1943. In S. Orwell & I. Angus (Eds.), *The collected essays, journalism, and letters of George Orwell*. New York: Harcourt, Brace, and World, Inc.

Paunesku, D., Walton, G. M., Romero, C., Smith, E. N., Yeager, D. S., & Dweck, C. S. (2015, April 10). Mind-set interventions are a scalable treatment for academic underachievement. *Psychological Science*, April 10, 1–10.

Pyc, M. A., Agarwal, P. K., & Roediger III, H. L. (2014). Test-enhanced learning. In V. A. Benassi, C. E. Overson, & C. M. Hakala (Eds.), *Applying science of learning in education: Infusing psychological science into the curriculum*. American Psychological Association Society for the Teaching of Psychology. Retrieved from http://www.teachpsych.org/Resources/Documents/ebooks/asle2014.pdf

Robins, R. W., & Pals, J. L. (2002). Implicit self-theories in the academic domain: Implications for goal orientation, attributions, affect, and self-esteem change. *Self and Identity, 1*(4), 313–336.

Roediger III, H. L., & Butler, A. C. (2007). Testing improves long-term retention in a simulated classroom setting. *European Journal of Cognitive Psychology, 19*, 514–527.

Roediger III, H. L., & Karpicke, J. D. (2006). The power of testing memory: Basic research and implications for educational practice. *Perspectives on Psychological Science, 1*, 181–210.

Rogerson, B. (2003). Effectiveness of a daily class progress assessment technique in introductory chemistry. *Journal of Chemical Education, 80*(2), 160–164.

Rohrer, D., & Taylor, K. (2007). The shuffling of mathematics problems improves learning. *Instructional Science, 35*(6), 481–498.

Schell, J. (2012, March 15). Peer instruction 101: What is peer instruction? *Turn to Your Neighbor: The Official Peer Instruction Blog.*

http://blog.peerinstruction.net/2012/03/15/peer-instruction-101-what-is-peer-instruction/

Talbert, R. (2014, April 28). Flipped learning skepticism: Is flipped learning just self-teaching? *Chronicle of Higher Education*. Retrieved from http://chronicle.com/blognetwork/castingoutnines/2014/04/28/flipped-learning-skepticism-is-flipped-learning-just-self-teaching/

Weimer, M. (2015, March 18). Using cumulative exams to help students revisit, review, and retain course content. *Faculty Focus*. Retrieved from http://www.facultyfocus.com/articles/teaching-professor-blog/using-cumulative-exams-help-students-revisit-review-retain-course-content/

Willingham, D. (2014). *Why don't students like school? A cognitive scientist answers questions about how the mind works and what it means for the classroom*. San Francisco: Jossey-Bass.

Wrzesniewsk, A., Schwartz, B., Cong, X., Kane, M., Omar, A., & Kolditz, T. (2014). Multiple types of motives don't multiply the motivation of West Point cadets. *Proceedings of the National Academy of Sciences of the United States of America, 111*(30), 10990–10995.

Yeager, D., Henderson, M., Paunesku, D., Walton, G., D'Mello, S., Spitzer, B., Duckworth, A. Boring but important: a self-transcendent purpose for learning fosters academic self-regulation. *Journal of Personality and Social Psychology 107*(4), 559–580.

Yuhas, D. (2014, October 2). Curiosity prepares the brain for better learning. *Scientific American*. Retrieved from http://www.scientificamerican.com/article/curiosity-prepares-the-brain-for-better-learning/

Zull, J. (2002). *The art of changing the brain: Enriching the practice of teaching by exploring the biology of learning*. Sterling, VA: Stylus.

Index